The best of

COBBWEBS

by Ty Cobb

Foreword by Rollan Melton
Edited by C.J. Hadley
With Kay Fahey

The Black Rock Press
The University of Nevada Foundation
University of Nevada, Reno
1997

Printed in the United States of America

The Black Rock Press
University Library/322
University of Nevada, Reno
Reno, NV 89557-0044

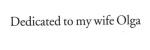
Dedicated to my wife Olga

Introduction

Bless our dear friend, Ty Cobb, the legendary Nevada journalist, for creating this literary jewel. "Best of Cobbwebs" is a wondrous collection of his *Reno Gazette-Journal* columns, and the representative work appearing here was created by him over nearly four decades.

In this, his first book, the reader is treated to Ty's enormous breadth of knowledge about his state; we see his wide-ranging grasp of rural and metropolitan Nevada; we are taken on a delightful journey to old Nevada, the one Ty Cobb first savored as a boy, and then as the young newspaperman fresh off the campus of the University of Nevada.

I first met one of my most beloved role models, Ty Cobb, in a telephone visit in 1948. I was a cub reporter for the weekly *Fallon Standard*, and as a high school junior, was responsible for phoning Ty long-distance with an account of a Sierra Sagebrush League baseball game. Though I could not then know it, I was speaking to the man who would become my outstanding mentor.

In each ensuing year since our first encounter, I have learned from Ty Cobb, master reporter and elegant writer. Readers of "Best of Cobbwebs" will learn from him, too. What we get here on each page is Ty's special gift of acquiring myriad detail, and then packaging it in a delightful style. The writing is compact; the storyline ever fascinating; the history inevitably reconstructed accurately, and with flair.

What a gorgeous journey Ty takes us on.

We acquire from him the delight of a boyhood spent in the Comstock: there is the famous Virginia City postmistress, Miss Katie O'Connor; we are transported into the legendary Piper's Opera House where there is an unexpected encounter with America's famous 20th century humorist, Will Rogers.

Ty Cobb makes past Nevada characters live again. Famous Wolf Pack football coach Jim Aikin's croaky voice is something akin to a bull's bellow; the famous nationally syndicated newspaper columnist, Westbrook Pegler, is squired around town by the young cub reporter, Ty Cobb—and remarkably, elects not to write negatively about Reno; Jake Lawlor, who was among Ty's best news sources, roars back to life, as the journalist creates a detailed portrait of the famous Nevada coach.

Even the non-sports fan will love Ty Cobb's telling of athletic lore. He tracks down Reno's Paul Beeler, who was the timekeeper at the famous Jack Dempsey-Gene Tunney "long count" heavyweight title fight; he regales us with baseball hijinks from old Moana Stadium; we are treated to a profile of former world's middleweight boxing contender Dick Evans—Ty takes us "ringside," as Evans manages his little Reno bar on East Fourth Street.

Foremost, Ty Cobb's love of history charms us. He delights with tales of his legendary namesake, the baseball hall of famer, Ty Cobb. We become witness, thanks to journalist Ty Cobb, to the fiery death of the Reno Country Club, destroyed in 1936; and the reader will meet many special Nevadans who would be lost in memory, except that Ty's gift for biography has made them live again.

As octogenarian, and despite his faltered vision, Ty Cobb remains today the supreme reporter and the optimist who invariably finds the good of society to chronicle. From 1937, when he left the campus and found his journalism calling, to this day, Ty Cobb remains a fresh voice on the printed page.

"Best of Cobbwebs" gracefully testifies to his gift of giving the reader his very best.

We are in the debt of this dearest Nevada friend. Long live Ty Cobb. The best of the best.

Rollan Melton
Reno Gazette-Journal

Foreword

A long time ago, in 1965 to be exact, Rollan Melton suggested to me that I write a column for the *Nevada State Journal*. (The *Journal* later was merged with the *Reno Evening Gazette* to become the *Reno Gazette-Journal*). The idea of a column had been recommended to me before, but I took Rollan's suggestion more seriously. After all, he was the *publisher* of the Reno Newspapers.

Rollan noted that I had the background to provide a worthy column. I had been born and raised in the old mining town of Virginia City, went to school in Reno and had a keen interest in Nevada history. Thus started what was actually my second foray into being a columnist, having earlier written a sports column for the *Nevada State Journal* for approximately 20 years, called *Inside Stuff*.

That was the start of *Cobbwebs*, a name that some of the printers at the *Journal* gave it. At first, I wrote three columns a week, despite my demanding duties as managing editor and head of the news room of a thriving paper. Later this was reduced to two a week, and after I retired in 1975 after some 38 years with the newspapers, I limited it to a once-a-week basis. The column still appears in the Sunday edition of the *Reno Gazette-Journal*.

In recent years, many friends urged me to write a book. Some meant an autobiography, others were insistent that I select some of the best columns for a book. "All you have to do is look over past columns and select some for a book." That was great advice, except that I have turned out more than *two thousand* Cobbwebs!

The newspapers' librarians had fortuitously clipped out my columns over the years and kept them in separate yearly envelopes, so I at least had access to the columns I had written. However, with my vision problems, extracting the better columns for inclusion in a book was a daunting and arduous task.

I was fortunate that Paul Page, Vice President of Development of the University of Nevada, arranged for the University of Nevada Foundation to coordinate this production, and C. J. Hadley was selected by the university to be the book's editor. This dynamic woman's background ranged from rodeo photographer to snowmobile racer toauthor-editor. She was publisher of *NEVADA Magazine*, and now is editor of the University of Nevada's Alumni magazine, *SILVER & BLUE*. In her "spare" time, she also publishes *RANGE*, about the "Cowboy Spirit on America's Outback."

Also of great assistance in preparation of this book were my son Ty, a former deputy National security advisor to President Reagan and current President of The Yosemite National Institutes, daughter, Patricia, an honor graduate of California State University, Los Angeles and former advertising executive; and my son, Bill Cobb, prominent Reno attorney and active University of Nevada alumnus.

The university arranged for Kay Fahey and Beverly Rivera to assist me. Kay was assistant editor. Beverly daily read a half-dozen columns aloud while I meditated and evaluated the candidate columns. Then I would give a yes or no, to save the best for the book. One day C.J. phoned me, declaring "You must be more ruthless. You have okayed enough for *three* books!"

Cobbwebs combines a myriad of subjects. Sports themes predominate, since I was sports editor for 22 years. My Virginia City background and growing up in Reno provided many topics, and my interest in Nevada history also appears frequently. Sometimes my subject is travel, as I have been fortunate enough to have cruised and toured a lot since retirement—about 15 foreign lands or distant U.S.A. domains. I tried to mingle this data with some humor, common sense, and memories.

On a personal note I would like to mention that several years ago I was honored by the university when I received its "Distinguished Nevadan Award," a recognition that I truly treasure. As a small token of my appreciation to the university and to the State of Nevada, I have requested that proceeds from the sale of *The Best of Cobbwebs* go to the general scholarship fund of my alma mater, the University of Nevada, Reno.

I thank all who have made this book a reality, particularly the University of Nevada for its support, and to my long time friend and contemporary Rollan Melton who penned a very gracious and thoughtful introduction to *Cobbwebs*. I hope this collection is as enjoyable to its readers as it has been to me in authoring the columns.

Ty Cobb
Reno, Nevada 1997

Contents

We traveled the streets of Virginia City, lustily singing Yuletide carols. 174

Their brass fittings gleamed, and disgorged great clouds of black smoke from the coal or wood-burning engines. 176

High jinks in the '30s. 178

It was the first time mainland Japan had been attacked. 179

If Proctor Hug started a carpet company, he could advertise "Hug's Rugs." 181

Only 1950's fans will remember a second-sacker for the Silver Sox. 184

Heavy make-up, heady perfume. 184

You had to have a good left hook add a line of leading to this one to qualify for the choice corner

Every time National Newspaper Week rolls around, and the energetic carrier boys are lauded for their good work, it stirs memories among us ex-carrier boys. Some of us can't forget our own days of delivering or selling Reno newspapers, no matter how long ago.

As a small boy, we used to envy the fellows who were lucky enough to acquire routes, but most particularly we envied the downtown paper sellers. We felt the acme of success was to be able to shout the papers' names from various street corners. (You had to have seniority, plus a good left hook, to qualify for the choice Virginia-Second corner, among others.)

There was a particular knack of calling *"Reno Even-ning Gaz-ETT*, Pay-PER!" The way those boys could make their voices go up and down on certain syllables was a touch of distinction. You had class if you could add that "Pay-PER" with proper emphasis. Unfortunately, the *"Nevada State Journal"* didn't have the tone combinations to be given similar vocal treatment. Also, the Journal came off the press after midnight, when small boys were supposed to be home sleeping.

Our first delivery job, however, was with an agency which distributed the big city papers in downtown Reno. We had the half of downtown east of Virginia Street. Lordy—how heavy those paper bags were when first loaded with *Examiners, Calls, Tribunes, Chronicles,*

> **VIGOROUS PROTEST**
>
> *The United Press reports this note from a ball game between a visiting semi-pro team and the inmates of a certain penitentiary: The manager of the "outside" team vigorously protested a decision by the umpire, who was an inmate. He bitterly questioned the umpire's judgment and honesty, but was silenced by the retort: "Look, Mac, if I was honest I wouldn't be here."*
> *—August 23, 1967*

the News, Bulletin and others! The man in charge helped place the double bags on our thin shoulders, and we lurched and staggered down Commercial Row until enough were delivered to lighten the load.

We hit the Big Time, however, when we landed a Journal delivery job. At that time, the papers weren't delivered, flat and unwrinkled, on the customer's front porch. They were rolled, tight and hard, to the consistency of a stick of wood. And bent in the center, to aid in throwing. What a toll they took of flowers, screens and windows!

Putting big business methods to work, we got together with the Beger brothers, who owned an old touring car and also delivered papers. We decided to combine forces in rolling the papers and carrying the routes together. Either Bev or Earl Beger drove the car, while the other continued rolling the papers and yours truly stood up in the back seat throwing them.

It worked beautifully; we covered all three routes in one-third the time. However, there was a residence on west California Avenue, past the bottom of the hill (out where the new Safeway Store stands now). The people had nice landscaping, and a flock of "pedigree" chickens. Some of the fowls were said to be exceedingly valuable.

One day, as we roared past this house, we didn't bother to slow or turn in the driveway. Just heaved the wadded-up paper like Carl Yazstremski throwing from the Boston outfield. And heard some loud squawks from the poultry.

Upon return to the newspaper office we were confronted by an irate circulation manager. He displayed a deceased fowl, draped limply on his desk. The three of us offered to make retribution, thinking two or three dollars was the going price at the poultry store. "Two dollars!" he roared, "This is a pedigreed, high-class, valuable chicken. It's more like fifty dollars!"

That concluded our association with newspaper delivery.

—October 15, 1967

Sometimes the old
wooden flumes were washed away

When we read in the Journal the other day about Virginia City's water-less period, we experienced a twinge of nostalgia. In our teen days—
and in the years before and years afterward—going without water for certain winter periods was an accepted way of life for the Comstockers.

Severe winter conditions have often plagued the mountain town's water lines. Sometimes the old wooden flumes were washed away or frozen tight. Little or no liquid came out of the faucets in the homes for days at a time, while the water company's crews labored manfully to restore the service.

Fortunately, the huge tanks higher on the mountain, which stored water for the fire mains, remained unfrozen. And the citizens drew upon the fire hydrants for enough of the wet stuff to use in cooking and dishwashing. Baths? Showers? Hah!

Many a crisp morning we trudged to the nearby fire hydrant at "A" and Union streets, with the neighbor boys, Eddie and Danny Connors. It was a cooperative plan. We filled those big tin boilers which were a vital part of every household and—puffing, grunting and moaning—made trip after trip back to our homes. How unbelievably heavy they were, and how those sharp handles cut into our hands! We filled our respective bath tubs, and every pot, pan, kettle and jar our parents could find.

With aching backs and bruised hands, we trudged to school, to study about water tables, rivers and brooks in our geography classes. After school there was another session with the fire hydrants. When the service was finally restored, the flow from the faucets and taps contained a goodly percentage of mud, twigs and ice fragments. But it was flowing, and the Hydrant Brigade had a respite.

—February 2, 1969

You can excuse the
memory of their swaggering walk

Who was your hero when you were a kid?

If you were a little lad in Reno or Elko in the '20s, your idol was the air mail pilot. You rode your bike out to the old airport—a one-hangar, tin-roofed affair at the end of a dusty cleared field. And you waited for the air mail plane to come in. It may have been a little late, but it usually arrived.

An open-cockpit biplane, generally a war surplus DeHaviland of World War I vintage. Single prop, with uncovered cylinders radiating in a circle. Sturdy struts connecting the two wings with wire bracing in between. Wire-spoke wheels. (A mechanic started the engine by hand-cranking the propeller.)

Those were the planes which braved the elements and scantily-charted routes of the West. And these were the pilots who flew them—Monte Mouton, Burr Winslow, Clare Vance, Harry Huking, Bill Blanchfield, J.W. Sharpnack, and others. Even Eddie Rickenbacker came through once in a while. Cracked up a plane hereabouts as did most of the others.

What romantic, dashing figures they were, in the eyes of their young admirers! Leather helmets and flying goggles. Leather jackets or loose coats with heavy fur collars. Baggy jodhpur pants and leather puttees. Some of the aviators affected small mustaches with carefully-waxed points.

You can excuse the memory of their swaggering walk. They earned the right to swagger. Battling through Sierra or Wasatch mountain snowstorms, trying to sight the few landmarks along the route without benefit of the magic radio beams, they were brave and intrepid men. —*April 14, 1968*

With Joe DiMaggio, sensational young outfielder and hitter for the New York Yankees. My first year on the Journal.

The weakest lady bowler
could have done a better job

We had been invited to roll the first ball for the official opening of the women's state bowling tourney. This invitation was accepted with grave misgivings. The smallest and weakest of the lady bowlers could probably have done a better job.

As the speeches went on, we became increasingly nervous. This would be a heck of a place to display our lack of skill, right in front of the state's standout keglers. Finally, with fanfare, we were called out on the alleys to trundle the "honorary first ball."

It dribbled weakly down the lane and plopped into the gutter on the right. They gave us another ball. In anxiety to correct the direction, we sent it spinning—to the left, and into that gutter. We wanted to hide behind the ten-pins; that was the safest place. Someone insisted we try a third time. This ball thundered—praise the Lord—right down the middle. Pow! a perfect strike!

The tourney committee, vastly relieved, swarmed around with congratulations. "That was sure a clever stunt, Mr. Cobb," commented one of the deceived ladies, "throwing those two gutter balls and then hitting a strike."

"We try to give 'em a little showmanship," we lied. And then hurried out the door before they could ask for a repeat.

—*April 28, 1968*

His newsboy never forgot him

A resident of southeast Reno, noting the "pajama delivery" ad in the Journal, called the circulation department and asked whether, as the ad said, he should get his paper by 7 a.m.

He was told he certainly should. The customer added that his newsboy was very good, never forgot him, but didn't get there until 7:30

a.m. A little later the subscriber again phoned the newspaper office, chuckling. He said he stopped the 12-year-old paper boy and showed him the ad. "It says here the Journal is to be delivered by 7 a.m."

The youngster studied the ad then commented, seriously, "I see that, mister, but you know, I didn't put that ad in the paper."

—June 28, 1968

Our yard literally rocked with the explosions of aerial bombs, the swoosh of skyrockets, and the hissing of blazing pinwheels

Last night's fireworks display at Mackay Stadium was public, spectacular, free and safe. And like the old western story about the man who complained about the shady roulette game but kept playing because it was "the only game in town," the Chamber of Commerce's pyrotechnics exhibition was also exclusive.

To a whole generation of young people, the managed, sanctioned displays at public stadiums have been their sole experience with fireworks. (Except for furtive shooting of "bootlegged" crackers.)

It wasn't like that when we were kids in the Reno of the late '20s and early '30s. Fireworks became a big thing in everyone's life. Hardly a house didn't have its own fireworks display. And the Cobb mansion did things up big. The Father of the House was really hooked on fireworks. We started planning weeks ahead of time when the illustrated catalogs arrived and we poured over pages of descriptions (and prices) of super skyrockets, Roman candles, and the rest. The family budget took a beating. The Mother of the House wistfully abandoned plans for a new vacuum cleaner, or even a broom; and the Boy chucked hopes for a new bicycle tire or baseball mitt. It was worth the sacrifices.

Excitement gripped the whole neighborhood when the express truck delivered the boxes of fireworks—clean wooden packages in which heaps of excelsior and straw padded the rockets and aerial bombs in transit.

Even the vast array strewn across the living room tables and floor wasn't enough. The Father of the House eventually concluded we'd better take a trip downtown to the Chinese stores on Lake Street to buy more supplies.

Our yard, and those of the neighbors, literally rocked with the explosions of aerial bombs, the swoosh of skyrockets, and the hissing of blazing pinwheels. For hours. We sought to aim the rockets in the general direction of the big empty lot at Wells, Wheeler and Crampton. Few got as far as the Rudolph Herz house, but some got off course and banged into the Jim Cusick and Bill Paterson homes. And John Brown often found burned-out aerial goodies in his corn patch. In turn, our own house and yard were visited by blazing, sparkling and banging missiles via the sky and from other July Fourth fans of the neighborhood.

It's a wonder half of Reno didn't burn up each Fourth. Or that half the kids (and dads) didn't get their fingers blown off, or hair burned off. If was a grand and glorious time—but not quite as safe and sane as Mackay Stadium's. —*July 5, 1968*

Tunney suddenly stopped and smashed Dempsey squarely in the mouth with a straight right

"Referee Dave Barry stood over Tunney, counting. Dempsey stood right there, too, ready to blast Tunney if and when he started to get up." That's how a figure in one of the sport's greatest and most controversial episodes recalls the "Night of the Long Count."

Paul Beeler now lives in Sparks. He retired as a railroader and moved from the hot and humid Sacramento Valley. The doctors told him the altitude and climate of the Reno area would benefit his health, so at the urging of old friend Robert Davis, Beeler and his wife moved here.

If you want a first-hand account of the famous Jack Dempsey-Gene Tunney fight in Chicago, you need seek no higher authority. There can't be any—Paul Beeler was the knockdown timekeeper at ringside in Soldiers Field, Chicago, Sept. 22, 1927.

That was the night 104,943 fans paid $2,658,660 to see ex-champion Dempsey attempt to regain the title from the ex-Marine who had dethroned him the year before, in Philadelphia. That was the night when Dempsey floored Tunney in the seventh round and hovered over him too long. Instead of retreating to "the fartherest neutral corner" as the then-new rules of boxing specified, Dempsey reverted to habit and/or instinct and stood over Tunney ready to belt him immediately.

Referee Barry saw him, halted his counting and literally wrestled the fiery Dempsey to the proper corner. Then he returned to the fallen champion and started counting—from one.

But timekeeper Paul Beeler had already tolled off several seconds, as he was supposed to do, from the moment Tunney hit the canvas. Altogether, Tunney got the benefit of an accumulated count of 14 seconds. Some observers thought it might have been even longer.

Could Tunney actually have risen before the designated ten-count?

"I am sure he could have," emphasizes time-keeper Paul Beeler. "I was so close to him I could have reached through the ropes and touched him. He was watching me count and his eyes were clear. He picked up my count and said 'six' with me.

"I know it would have been rough on Tunney had he arisen right then. But he was smart. He took advantage of the extra time. When he got up he 'got on his bicycle'—retreating and sticking his left glove in Dempsey's face. Dempsey was infuriated. He couldn't catch Gene. He swore and growled for Tunney to fight. But Jack was tiring. His legs were weary. Then Tunney suddenly stopped and smashed Dempsey squarely in the mouth with a straight right. He did it again and that was it. Tunney was back in command. Dempsey couldn't catch up any more."

The rules of boxing used to permit a scrapper to stand over a knocked-down opponent and slug him as he tried to regain his feet. Often the downed victim never got to his haunches or knees before he was bashed. The Dempsey-Firpo fight precipitated a change in ring rules—the neutral corner bit.

"Actually, Dempsey had no excuses in this episode. The commission put emphasis on this particular rule. In the pre-fighting meeting at headquarters, they 'laid the law down' specifically to Dempsey. And Jack said he understood. . . He just got excited in the ring," explained Beeler.

Paul Beeler was the timekeeper for innumerable bouts in the 1920s, when the ring game was really thriving. "In my book," Beeler reminisces, "Jack Dempsey was the greatest of all heavyweights. He could hit, he was fast and he could take it... But, pound-for-pound, Harry Greb (light-heavyweight) was the best I ever saw."

Paul Beeler is far from Chicago's Soldiers Field now, far from the clang of the gong and the roar of the crowd. But he has a memory of one of the most exciting sports dramas of all time, because he was a part of it. —*Sunday, June 1, 1969*

After some losing blackjack and evil whiskey, Mr. Pegler settled for two bags of peanuts in lieu of dinner

Death of famous columnist Westbrook Pegler was reported the other day, and it reminded quite a few persons that Pegler's syndicated column was carried in the Nevada State Journal of the 1930s and early '40s.

He was the most-feared writer of his time, and his vitriolic words seared the hides of politicians, Supreme Court justices, Presidents and their wives. There really wasn't much that Pegler had a good word for.

Thus it was with dismay that we of the Journal staff learned that Mr. Pegler was visiting Reno. "Gosh, we hope he can find something nice to say about our town," was the consensus.

Things were not conducive to a good impression of Reno. It was the heart of winter and times were extremely dull. Instead of the glamorous Divorce Capital which was famous nationwide, it was pretty ordinary that weekend. Cold, and a steady drizzle of rain. Mr. Pegler visited one "glamour spot" and got served some bad whiskey, also lost every hand of blackjack he played. He was not in a good mood when he visited the Journal office, where everyone but a couple

Walter Winchell, famous broadcaster and columnist from New York. On the right, Wilbur Clark, owner of the Desert Inn resort in Las Vegas. The occasion was the Tournament of Champions golf classic.

of "cubs" had finished work and departed. He commanded us to accompany him to "dinner." But by that time just about all the good cafes had closed. After some more losing blackjack and evil whiskey, Mr. Pegler settled for two bags of peanuts in lieu of dinner.

He sat there moodily staring out at the dismal rainy night, and we silently faded away, un-noticed.

Next day our staff compared notes. "This is awful. He had a rotten time. Bet Pegler writes a sizzling expose of Reno. He'll tear our hide off."

Day after day we rushed to the Pegler column to see how he vented his acid on Reno. It was even worse; he never wrote a word about Reno. —*Wednesday, July 2, 1969*

We could barely distinguish the announcer's words amid the blather of squawks, roars and hums from the radio

During the recent Homecoming-Reunion of the Fourth Ward School alumni in Virginia City, one of the leading figures was that of burly, ruddy-faced Ted Beckett, probably the most famous athlete ever produced on the Comstock Lode.

Now retired and living in Reno, Beckett retains almost legendary prestige among the "Hot Water Plugs." In the mid 1920s, he was a basketball stalwart at Virginia City High School, also a boxer of note, having fought a few 10 rounders.

It was at the University of California, however, that Ted Beckett gained the most fame. Partly as a heavyweight boxer (and teammate of the late Cal coach Ed Nemir) but mostly as a football guard of such ability that, on a weak Golden Bear team, he won All-America honors in the early 1930s.

DEBONAIR FLACK

Art Long, debonair flack for the (Greater) Reno Chamber of Commerce, has that "freshly scrubbed" look this week. It's because he drove his auto into one of those Reno automatic car washes, the kind where the driver remains inside the vehicle while the sprays and brushes slosh and whisk away. And he left his window open.
—April 3, 1968

We who were then youngsters on the Comstock at the time regarded Ted Beckett as a folk hero and eagerly scanned the daily papers for any mention of our erstwhile fellow townsman. And on Saturday afternoons we were literally glued to the loud speakers of our radio sets, listening to the University of California football broadcasts.

Reception was none too good, and for some strange reason, there was an unusual amount of static on Saturday afternoons. We could barely distinguish the announcer's words. "Did he say Ted Beckett made the tackle?" we would ask each other amid a blather of squawks, roars and hums from the radio.

Some of the more observing youngsters discovered that (this was just before the end of the Prohibition Era) a gentleman living at the north side of town supplemented his income by producing home-made booze. It was so fresh that he "aged" the product with the aid of an electric gadget known as the "needle." Unfortunately, the "needle" interfered with radio reception, generating ear-splitting static which blotted out the University of California grid broadcasts.

A delegation of the lads called on the whiskey manufacturer and laid down an ultimatum—either he suspend his electric needle during the Cal football games or they'd turn him in to the "prohis" (prohibition enforcement agents).

The deal was made. The bootlegging activity was halted on Saturday afternoons, the Cal grid games came in loud and clear, and the young fellows got to hear numerous mentions of their idol, Ted Beckett.—*Sunday, May 11, 1969*

Impressing a young cutie with sophisticated conversation

We've been doing some thinking about Bing Crosby lately, since a feature story appeared in a recent Nevada State Journal. And we realized that our one-time hostility toward the King of the Crooners had mellowed into tolerance, nay, even admiration.

Probably our first reactions to Bing Crosby were the same experienced by millions of young men in ensuing years in connection with Frank Sinatra, Elvis Presley, and the Beatles. Disruption and jealousy. Bing "beat our time" back in the 1930s even though he never approached Virginia City. Something about his throaty octaves turned the young ladies into jelly.

It happened every afternoon along about 4 o'clock.

We were making good progress with a certain young cutie, impressing her by our sophisticated conversation about the previous weekend's baseball game with Gardnerville, or sparkling tidbits about the upcoming Golden Gloves boxing tournament.

Wide-eyed, she gave us flattering attention. Until the clock gave warning that the hour of four was approaching. Then a look of alarm and anxiety would replace the spell we had cast. "Oo, oo, oo—it's time for Bing!" she would exclaim. All over the town. And, we are sure, all over the country, many other sweet young things were blacking out their boy friends and zeroing in on Bing's broadcast.

Once the Groaner came through with "When the blue of the night meets the gold of the day" the gals were goners. So were the boy friends. The starry-eyed damsels gradually returned to normal about an hour or two after Bing signed off. Then it was too late. The boys had all gone home to dinner or baseball practice.

Many years later the image of Bing Crosby as a movie comedian, race horse fancier and baseball backer served to erase our early animosity. And when Bing moved to Nevada, working cattle on his Elko County ranch, his prestige gained a notch. "Just a regular guy," the Elko folks would insist. Bing preferred to talk cattle, branding, beef prices and such and wanted to camouflage his movie star aura beneath a set of dusty denims. The Elko people realized that and treated him "like one of the guys." No one pestered him for autographs or to sing at benefits.

But one time he did sing at a benefit. In fact, he sang all night. There was some worthy local cause and Bing agreed to come in and sing for it. He put on the whole show—master of ceremonies, comedian and songster. The Commercial Hotel was jammed—the show room, the hallways, adjacent rooms, even the sidewalks. Had such a one-man show been produced now as a Bing Crosby Special on national TV it would be a million dollar production.

The bartenders and dealers staged their second annual game (softball) at Moana Park, replete with gags, stunts and top entertainment. It was for a good cause, the Eagle Valley Children's Home. The year before, the bartenders and dealers put on a similar affair for the benefit of the Spokane ball club. That team's bus plunged off a cliff, killing or seriously injuring most of the players. Special benefits were staged throughout the country, but the Reno bartenders and dealers raised the biggest sum, something like $4,000.

Bing knew about this, since Spokane was his home town and baseball was his hobby. So when the second annual Reno bartender-dealer game was staged, the Groaner not only agreed to attend but volunteered to play. In fact, he appeared in the uniform of the Pittsburgh Pirates (of which he was part-owner). Played a good brand of ball too, and frolicked a little. We recall that when Pete Barengo was beaned by a fly ball, Crosby administered first aid, pouring a flagon of beer on the victim's aching head.

Oh, yes. About that article in last week's Journal which started all this: it mentioned that Bing Crosby had reached the tender age of 65 and was qualified for Medicare. Not that Mr. Crosby, a millionaire several times over, will ever need government aid for his aspirins and band-aids. But we just realized that we're not mad at Bing any more.

—*Sunday, May 18, 1969*

Coach Aiken's most gentle conversation voice was comparable to a bull's bellow

Marion Motley was a University of Nevada all-time great football star, and a professional (Cleveland Browns) luminary. We'll remember Motley for his athletic feats, also as a prodigious sleeper.

One time he told us he could utilize 12 to 14 hours of sleep per day, and we presume this slumber was one factor in re-charging his athletic batteries, giving him that tremendous energy on the gridiron. Class schedules somewhat interfered with this program. Marion, in later years liked to re-tell the time he dozed off during one of Prof. Higginbotham's lectures, seat tilted back against a steam radiator in the back of the room, and his feet wedged to the bottoms of two empty chairs in front. Mot not only dozed off, but he dreamed. And he dreamed of playing football. His feet churned furiously, agitating the two empty chairs, then he tipped over backwards with a crash. His head smacked against the steam radiator. "Worse than any tackle I ever felt on the field," he recalled.

Another Motley feat was sleeping through a Jim Aiken chalk talk. This was no mere trick, either. Coach Aiken's most gentle conversation voice was comparable to a bull's bellow. It was rasping and penetrating. The night before a big game Aiken assembled the squad before a blackboard and went over the plays.

He stared suspiciously at Marion, perched on a rear seat with a baseball cap jammed over his eyes and chewing several sticks of gum. Coach Jim roared his instructions, then exhorted the team to go out the next day and win for good old Nevada. The inspired, or relieved, players scampered away. All but the unflappable Motley, who was nudged into wakefulness by a buddy, and arose, yawned and trotted home to bed. He had a great game the next day.

—*Sunday, July 6, 1969*

As an urchin, we approached the window in a timid and awestruck manner

A new building of any kind is news on the Comstock, where historical-minded citizens are trying desperately to preserve remnants of the colorful 19th century architecture. They are thankful the government architects didn't design the new post office in plastic and polished steel, and designate it with a neon sign.

The many visitors to Virginia City "relate" to Piper's Opera House, the Brass Rail, Bucket of Blood and similar landmarks, but they are less familiar with the post office as a holdover from the Bonanza Days.

The late and great writer Lucius Beebe, who was enamored of the Comstock, wrote one of his finest articles about the Virginia City post office and the traditional social hour which preceeded the arrival and distribution of mail.

He noted that social life of Virginia City began daily with the presence of the courthouse people, who had first crack at the new deliveries, and the rest of the folks used the occasion to discuss politics and the damp events of the previous night.

We have a few memories which pre-date those of the late Mr. Beebe, who had to live on the Comstock about 15 years before he stopped being regarded as a Johnny-Come-Lately.

We recall the former premises in the huge and ornate Marye Building, which was destroyed by fire in 1950. It was a dark and austere place, the floors heavily oiled and with an atmosphere which literally commanded visitors to speak in whispers, as in a church. As an urchin, we approached the window in a timid and awestruck manner. Even when standing on the little box which Postmaster Mike Nevin thoughtfully provided for small boys, we couldn't see eye-to-eye with the postmaster—a kindly and dignified gentleman with a huge walrus mustache. It was a mark of distinction to have this imposing official look down from the window and call us by name. This created envy among our fellow moppets, who forgot that Mr. Nevin also lived across the street from our house.

Later he was succeeded by Miss Katie O'Connor, a bustling lady with a commanding voice, who could be heard calling instructions to her aides as they distributed mail to the little postal boxes. We peered through the small glass windows of the boxes and hoped Miss O'Connor would shortcut her chores and stuff mail into Box 395.

Mr. Beebe was correct in noting the post office was the focal point of Comstock life. The mail and lunch hour were synonymous, during our prep years. We knew lunch time was approaching by two signs, the hunger pangs in our stomach and the whistle of the V&T train as it climbed the Gold Hill grade and neared the Divide. From windows of the Fourth Ward School we could watch the Ward Tunnel southeast of Virginia City and see a billow of white smoke emerge from the tunnel a second ahead of the puffing V&T locomotive.

By the time school was dismissed for the noon hour we knew that Arthur (Audie) Dick was urging his horse-drawn dray alongside the Virginia & Truckee yellow baggage-mail cars and taking aboard cargo. Lest you think this era dates back to the John Mackay days, we hasten to point out that certain merchants clung to horse-drawn wagon delivery up into the 1940s.

By the time we reached the post office Mr. Audie Dick was unloading his cargo, and we sacrificed part of the lunch hour to wait for the mail to be distributed. The Nevada State Journal was a must before lunch, especially Henry McLemore's column. And the postal box contents usually included items to delight a boy's heart—the *Boy's Life* magazine, letters from pen pals around the country and in foreign countries, and sometimes those wonderful catalogs from novelty firms.

The Johnson-Smith catalog was the greatest delight, as it advertised 4,000 items including disappearing ink, hand buzzers, a gadget which ostensibly would permit you to "throw" your voice (the illustration showed a boy's voice coming from a trunk, mystifying the man carrying it), and other marvels at a bargain price. A few years later we were all more interested in scented envelopes in feminine handwriting and sporting goods catalogs and not yet expecting arrival of official-looking envelopes containing Greetings from the President of the United States.

At any rate, we are pleased the post office has returned to the original site, the Marye Building location. Postmaster Tex Gladding notes that since the burned-out post office was moved several doors down "C" Street to the old California Bank office, it was designated in official correspondence from the postal department as a "temporary site." That was in 1950.—*Sunday, July 13, 1969*

The iron trough had a green, moss-like growth clinging to its innards

Gold Hill (actually a canyon) is on the road from Silver City to Virginia City. It used to be a challenge for the automobiles of some years back to pull lower Gold Hill in high gear, or even second gear, as far as Hoskings' trough.

The Hoskings family had a home back from the road, with a lush fruit orchard in front of it. And on the road was an old iron trough, always filled with sparkling clear water. Half of the cars' radiators would be boiling and steaming by the time they reached Hoskings' place, so it was a welcome stop.

The radiators were replenished with the trough water, and the passengers usually slurped a drink of the cold liquid which was said to originate in a spring behind the house. "One of the very few springs to be found on the Comstock Lode," where the deep mines drained off just about all surface water.

The iron trough had a green, moss-like growth clinging to its innards, but this didn't seem to affect the flavor of the spring water, nor the health of a large bullfrog who also dwelt there. A good coating of golden-colored rust added a little "body" to the liquid.

Now, Hoskings' house is gone. Most of the fruit orchard has dried up and is barren. The watering trough was still alongside the road, discarded, last time we looked. But it was disconnected from the pipe which used to discharge that sparkling spring water into the iron container, and was bone-dry and forlorn.

We're not sure how far back this watering trough dates, but the old-timers say they always stopped their buggies and wagons there to give the horses a rest and a refreshing drink. And we don't know how many generations of Comstockers grew up on the legend of the sparkling spring water. But we heard that when the place was torn down, it was discovered that instead of coming from an underground source as a spring, the water had been trickling into the pipe from an ancient leak in the community water main, for lo, these many, many years.

So the tradition, along with the water trough, has dried up, too.

—*Sunday, August 17, 1969*

They struck up a conversation, and the subject turned to boxing

Jimmy Olivas, coach of the University of Nevada boxing team, was getting his hair cut at the barbershop in Cal-Neva Lodge, Lake Tahoe. The barber was Cecil Beazley. They struck up a conversation, as is the custom in a barber shop, and the subject turned to boxing.

Barber Beazley mentioned that he used to be an amateur boxer. Customer Olivas said he was, too. Beazley said he got as far as the Far

Western championship tournament at Portland, Ore. Olivas said he also competed in the same tournament.

Waving his comb and scissors in delight, the barber said: "That was in 1929. That the same year you were in it?" Casually flicking some hair clippings from the sheet over his shoulders, customer Olivas conceded it was the same tournament, 40 years ago. Perhaps in relief that the barber was wielding a comb, and not a razor, the customer added, "Well, I won the welterweight division."

A good sport, the barber conceded, "I was a welterweight, too, and you beat me." Then barber Beazley rummaged through a drawer under the shelf which supported his hair tonics and brushes, and produced a photo which verified that both barber Beazley and customer Olivas had, indeed, been opponents in that Portland tournament 40 years ago.— *October 31, 1969*

Those dusty summer days back in the early '30s

A few weeks ago Leslie Burns Gray, tri-ply politico-barrister-scribe, issued a dire threat in his weekly column, which is about the last remnant of Comstock-originated journalism in the Virginia City-based *Territorial Enterprise.*

In his next column, he vowed, he'd reap a long-delayed revenge on the *Journal's* Ty Cobb for a dirty trick dating back to our high school days. LBG intimated that his Sparks baseball nine was done wrong when it came to the Comstock on those dusty summer days back in the early '30s.

We waited with some trepidation for the next issue of the *Enterprise*, but there was no Les Gray column. Not because of censorship, but because somehow the copy got mis-routed in the mails. Eventually, the copy did arrive and the column finally was printed. We breathed easier, because the latest wearer of the mantle of Mark Twain really dealt with us kindly. He was complimentary in touting us above the legendary Lucius Beebe. He even went back to one of the first Cobb articles—on Dan DeQuille—and said he couldn't locate it in a search of all the Nevada (highway) Magazines of the '30s. That was because it was published in the Nevada State Prison magazine—the *Rainbow*, instead of the highway issue.

How an article by a high school student from Virginia City came to be printed in a penitentiary publication is an unusual one. Our fledgling journalistic efforts were confined to writing up various sand-lot baseball and football games, in the weekly *Virginia City News,* predecessor to the latter-day *Territorial Enterprise.*

We had a relative, employed in the office of the Nevada State Prison, and he mentioned there that he had a nephew who was starting out as a writer. This came to the attention of a trusty in the prison office, an inmate whose behavior was so straight and whose literary ability was so sharp that he also doubled as editor of the convicts' magazine, the Rainbow.

He volunteered to provide journalistic coaching, so every few days we made the trek down to the prison and in the trusty's spare time, which was considerable, he assumed the role of an instructor. The man knew his stuff (his *Rainbow* magazine was one of the finest of its kind in the country) and his youthful protégé was given groundwork in the art of writing. We progressed to the point where he began placing our contributions in the prison magazine, although we didn't meet the resident qualifications as staffer. Hence the aforementioned Dan DeQuille piece which Leslie Gray referred to.

Unfortunately, our relation with the trusty-editor was only temporary. His instruction was interruped by a sudden departure. The gentleman's skills in writing were not confined to stories and articles; he was a clever penman concerning checks. Hence his confinement in the Carson pokey. His manners were flawless and his attitude sincere. He was also known as a Con Man.

Somehow, he let word leak out that he had learned from other convicts the location of a buried treasure. This was ostensibly loot from some bank robbery or other caper, and it had been stashed away in the mountains of a nearby California county.

Through the grapevine, this tip, as it was intended, reached the ears of a California sheriff, who made a trip to the Nevada pen and asked the warden if he could borrow his office trusty.

This was accomplished, and they trekked into the foothills in search of the buried treasure. Sometime later, the part-time Con Man said he had trouble spotting certain landmarks. He suggested that he would climb the mountain in one direction while the lawman assayed a different route.

Shortly afterward, the convict-editor-guide reversed his direction and went the other way—down the mountain to where the police car was parked. And away he went!

Even when the car broke down on a sandy road his luck held out. Passing motorists were persuaded that the sheriff had broken a leg and the Con Man was on the way for help. They even gave him a ride to Gardnerville.

From here, the trail dimmed momentarily. He next appeared at Puget Sound where he took a ride in a motor yacht, on a trial-purchase cruise. His work in the prison office, and skill in penmanship, made it easy to duplicate the signature of the prison clerk-purchasing officer.

With these credentials, he was greeted warmly by manufacturers eager to win a big order from the Nevada Prison. They were only too willing to advance personal credit and cash to the "purchasing agent." He dressed well, dined well, lived well—and moved on. Often the manufacturers did get their orders. The barnstorming Con Man appeared in Minnesota, Arkansas, all over. He bought a set of football uniforms for the convicts. He ordered a gross of steel cells for the prison. He even sent a telegram to the Nevada governor, asking him to put more money in the prison fund so he could make some better purchases.

Eventually, the Long Arm of the Law caught up with the debonair ex-Editor and Buried Treasure Guide. In New York. We went to the Reno depot when he was returned. He looked quite different from the smooth, sincere journalistic tutor we had known. Handcuffed, in leg irons, unshaven and dejected.

His next stop was the Warden's solitary dungeon, so we did not ask him for any more journalism classes.—*December 21, 1969*

Bloody noses and black eyes
were standard with the infielders

The topic of Virginia City's baseball ground rules was originally stimulated by some dour comments by Leslie Burns Gray who intimated that he and his Sparks baseball teammates were "jobbed" when they visited the Comstock for a game a long, long time ago. Since he's a lawyer as well as a political columnist, we plead *nolo contendere* (no contest) to his insinuations.

Yes, the Sparks boys were a bit baffled by conditions at the old Pan Mill diamond, but we didn't just spring the regulations out of thin air. Several previous generations of Comstockers had also played on the Pan Mill, and the ground rules were made necessary by physical conditions. Few baseball parks in the world had such a terrain.

The Pan Mill was a baseball field because it was the only sizable semi-level piece of ground in Virginia City, which, you know, is situated on the side of a large and steep mountain. Its name came because originally a mill stood on the site back in the Bonanza Days of the previous century. When it was utilized first for baseball we can't discover, but they were playing ball on the site as far back as the Gay '90s.

The Pan Mill was located east of Virginia City proper, which means below the town; north of the C&C (Consolidated Virginia & California) bonanza mine; and west of the old brewery which has more recently been converted into a monastery by members of a yoga cult.

Home plate was situated rather close to the backstop, and any high foul balls were destined to sail over the backstop and land on the road going down the Six Mile Canyon. Many hit this steep road and rolled swiftly down the Canyon, past the brewery and when last seen were heading in the direction of Sugar Loaf Mountain, miles below.

Third base was slightly shaded by two large poplar trees, but the third baseman didn't have much range. Only 10 or 15 feet to the east the field suddenly dropped off, down a steep bank to a side road below. The home town boys had the safe distance memorized and usually stopped pursuit of foul fly balls just in time. Unwary visiting

Jim Thorpe was a great Indian athlete. Winner of numerous Olympic gold medals, he became a major league baseball pitcher and NFL football star.

infielders were known to have plunged over the edge and rolled 20 feet down the bank.

On the other hand, the right side of the field was bordered by tall and steep mine dumps (where the non-productive dirt taken out of the old-time mines had been deposited back in the 1860s and '70s). Immediately behind first base a part of the mine dump rose steeply, giving the first baseman only about 10 feet behind the bag in which to operate.

Some of the home town first-sackers had a knack of playing "bank shots" as line drives in that direction caromed off the dump.

There was little more leeway in right field, however, as the contour of the mine dumps receded a bit there. Since there were no grandstands or bleachers, at least in the 1930s, the first-base mine dump was a favorite vantage point for spectators. Particularly, the Indian residents of the Comstock liked to perch there, high above the field, and look over the action.

Center field had more territory in which the outfielders could roam, hampered only by a fringe of sagebrush and an elderly but solid telephone pole. But left field—ah, that was something else. Deep left field dipped into lower ground which was further obscured by a tall crop of sagebrush. Thus when a leftfielder pursued a long fly ball in the direction of the C&C mine surface workings, he vanished from view of the other players and the umpires. Quite often, the outfielder would return, flourishing a baseball over his head, to indicate he had made a miraculous catch.

Who could deny it? No one could see what transpired out there in that low, brush-covered region. Well, not everyone. The folks perched atop the lofty mine dump behind first base had a bird's-eye view of the entire field. One time an outfielder—we believe he was a Lovelock fellow—returned from the outer limits triumphantly brandishing a baseball. "Batter's out," ruled the umpire, in lieu of better evidence. Whereupon a large Indian lady who was seated atop the first base dump arose, made her way down the steep bank, strode across the infield and confronted the umpire. "He's a —— —— liar!" she advised the arbiter. "He never caught any ball." Without another word, she turned, padded back across the infield and up the mine dump, in triumph over righting a wrong.

Many a baseball hit into the hinterlands of left field vanished into the brush. In the 1930s, young Italo Gavazzi whose home was nearby made himself a good piece of change by uncovering lost baseballs and selling them back to the home club.

The Pan Mill diamond produced some marvelous fielding gems and mishaps, too. It was no Moana Park as to green turf. There was no turf. Just quartz fragments and dust. Geologists will tell you the Comstock Lode's deposits of gold and silver were largely contained in quartz rock. Much of the Pan Mill baseball field was covered with lumps, slivers and sharp, though minute, pieces of quartz.

It did little good to groom the infield. Generations of Comstock ball players worked on the surface with graders, scrapers and hand rakes. To no avail. It looked good after such a smoothing, but minutes after being churned by players' spikes or a sharp wind (the Washoe Zephyrs blew across the Pan Mill, carrying off the surface dust) a crop of sharp quartz particles made their appearance. They came back up faster than corn grows in Iowa.

Almost every ground ball took strange bounces when hit onto this surface—veering down, up or sideways but seldom straight into a waiting glove.

Bloody noses and black eyes were standard with the infielders. These conditions were probably what have remained vivid in the memory of Leslie Burns Gray these many years, and it's not true that the Hilltoppers made strange ground rules to confound the visitors. It was just because we were more accustomed to the lunar-like terrain than the visitors were.

It is also not true that our home town clubs hid a convenient supply of extra baseballs under the sagebrush in the "out of sight" left field, so that if a fly ball was lost, there was always a substitute baseball ready.—*Sunday, January 11, 1970*

After a fanfare from the band, the massive Anderson started to hoist the apparatus

Charles Mapes, host at a cioppino feed the other night, was reminiscing about people and events at the Sky Room and decided an incident involving the world's strongest man was the capper.

Paul Anderson, fresh from his weight-lifting triumph in the Olympics, was attempting an unbelievable feat. He stood in the middle of the stage with a harness arrangement from his shoulders attached to a circular platform (it looked like a playground merry-go-round). Several of the band members perched on the platform, then some chorus girls and a couple of waiters. Nearly a dozen persons, as we recall.

After a fanfare from the band, the massive Anderson started to hoist the apparatus—musicians, chorus girls and all. Grunting and huffing, veins swelling in his forehead and neck, he lifted the entire entourage off the floor. Most spectacular lift of its kind in history. But a matter of seconds.

A photographer rushed up to capture the historic moment on film. Click, went the shutter. But the flash bulb failed. "Hey, Paul," he asked. "Hold it a minute until I get another flash bulb."

Anderson gamely held his stance, although the stage floor started to give away under the mighty load, until the photo was taken.

—March 22, 1970

A burning question

Who do you think was one of the first draft card burners?

We can't verify the actual first, but J.E. (Doc) Martie could well have been the initial American who torched his military draft literature.

Wait a minute—before you scream: "Doc Martie? The national American Legion official? The much-decorated hero of World War I?"

Doc Martie was the one who told us, so it must be true. Fifty-two years ago Martie—one of the first volunteers for the U.S. Expeditionary Force—was in the front line trenches in France. He had just come through two tremendous battles against the Germans, and performed so staunchly he was made an officer, on the spot, and given a battlefield commission.

The weary young lieutenant was sitting in the trench when the first mail in many days arrived. He looked at his, an official-looking envelope from his home town. It was a notice from his draft board, telling Martie to report for induction. "I looked at it for a few minutes, then touched a match to it. Didn't think they'd really mind."

—April 19, 1970

They battered each other in a torrid prize fight

The recent Tonopah Picnic in Reno brought about numerous reunions of old friends. But none was more surprising and sentimental than the get-together of Lawrence Zeni, who drove all the way from Seattle, and Clyde Hedrick of Mina.

They greeted each other like long-lost brothers. The last time they got together was in the ring in Tonopah in 1925 when they battered each other in a torrid prize fight.

Hedrick, a veteran of the ring, was then a miner and Zeni was the town's ice man. Lawrence concedes he lost the bout, "But it might have been different if I hadn't worked delivering cakes of ice until just before time for the fight."

He suffered a badly damaged ear in the scrap, and went home in misery. Guess who came to his house to administer first aid? Opponent Clyde and his second. Fixed him up like new.

—August 28, 1970

Another kind of Bethlehem

This happened before Christmas, but the story has just drifted down to Reno from Lassen County.

They tell us there was a school play being presented in connection with the Yule time, and all the parents and neighbors gathered, in a little rural community near Susanville. One young fellow had only one line to deliver. He had the role of the inn-keeper at Bethlehem, and when Joseph came to the door and inquired about a room for the night, the young host was supposed to answer: "No, we have no rooms left tonight."

He delivered the negative line all right, but added " . . . but would you like to come in for a cocktail?"

—February 6, 1970

After the final game the Journal *one-mansports staff had to make a dash for the parking lot*

The high school basketball tournament is in full swing today in Reno, and we're pleased that the *Nevada State Journal* sports staff, augmented by a crop of part-time scribes, is giving its usual thorough coverage to the event.

The operation makes a little more sense than it did during our earlier years on the *Journal*, in the role of a one-man sports staff. For various reasons, chiefly economic and personnel-wise, we attempted to cover all the tournament games single-handed for several years.

This included: getting up to the university gymnasium in time for the 9 a.m. games (we kept a play-by-play account and a running scorebook) and the last tilt wasn't over until 10:30 or 11 p.m. During the interval between games, when the new teams were warming up, there was time to total up and type out the previous box score, verify it with the official scorer, and get lineups for the ensuing contest. At halftime, while the bands were blaring, rooters cheering and old friends dropping by the press box to chat, we attempted to type the story of the previous game. There was also an occasional interview on radio, to eat up more time.

At the lunch and dinner hour breaks, we'd dash downtown to the newspaper office, write headlines and work on layouts for the up-coming morning edition (press time midnight). Then back to the gym to resume coverage of the everlasting tournament. There were also brief breaks in which to visit the coaches hospitality room and gab with tourney team mentors and others—picking up little items to pad out a daily tournament "sidelight" column.

Oh yes—we were also shepherding the photographer and lining up every team for group photos, and gathering identification for the captions. This wasn't always easy. Some coaches were superstitious about their teams being photographed before games (bad luck, you know) and it was also a chore to line up squads for pictures just after the games; they were either whooping it up because they won or morosely grumping about losing.

After the final game the Journal one-man sports staff had to make a dash for the parking lot, wriggle through the traffic jam of departing fans, and zoom back to the newspaper office. Then came another frantic round of headlining the last stories, filling out the tournament brackets for the printers, rushing late UPI copy, selecting action photos and writing captions—all to be completed before the ultimate 11:30 p.m. deadline! A "must" was a new comprehensive lead in results of the day and night and advancing the next day's competition.

Saturday night was probably the most demanding. After disposing with the afternoon (consolation finals) games, we prepared and distributed ballots for all-state tournament selections at half-time of the "B" division final. At half-time of the big-school final game, we again fought our way through the crowds, hunted up coaches, newsmen and others who had the all-star ballots—then we had to compile the votes.

Within a few minutes after the final buzzer of the last game, presentation of trophies would begin. We'd barely finish tallying the all-star team votes, scrambled again through the jumping crowd, and reach the microphone just as Neil Scott or whoever was the tourney director was calling on us to announce the all-stars and present them with their gold and silver basketballs (now forbidden by state athletic league officials).

Then, hi ho for the newspaper office again, as the clock ticked closer to deadline time. A broken typewriter ribbon or a flat tire were sheer catastrophe.

It wasn't for several years of the madness that we wised up and got some help to keep the scorebook, etc., and even later had aid from Bruce Shelley, Frenchy Laxalt, Rollan Melton and many others in typing the box scores and covering some of the games.

The pressure was still massive, however, but it was relieved later when the *Journal* expanded to a two-man sports staff and we had Len Crocker to lighten the load. Strangely enough, it was not until three years after we departed the sports desk completely that we suffered our coronary. Delayed reaction, no doubt.

The possible record for coverage, however, was hung up by Gib Landell when he went to the state tournament, at Las Vegas, a few years ago (when there were four divisions of schools) and he covered and telephoned a total of 12 games in one day!

Telephoning all the box scores and stories to the *Journal* from the daylight session took over an hour and, Landell pointed out, he was fortunate to have a helper on hand. "By the time we'd completed the marathon phone call," Landell said, "we had nearly lost our voices. After half a sandwich in the Convention Center and a hurried cup of coffee, we heard the buzzer sounding for the evening-session opener."

Now, the Journal coverage makes more sense. Gib Landell, with aides Gary Rawlings and Tom Dye and a retinue of part-timers, has a system of rotating assignments and a different writer covers each game, then hustles back to the office to write his story and box score. It's more efficient and easier on the nervous system, but no matter how many persons are assigned to the mammoth sports events, it's still a hectic job. We still like the games but somehow we don't miss that single-handed stuff one bit.—*March 12, 1971*

The miner was betting his wages on Sunday's game

During a talk session one night in Hawthorne the subject drifted to semi-pro baseball and the rivalry of Nevada mining camps to outdo each other.

Back in the late 1930s one mine at Round Mountain sought to recruit a good ball club and induced a number of college athletes to spend their summer there. The enticement was an offer of a job, and in those days of scanty employment such a bid was sufficient.

Among the University of Nevada athletes recruited by the ambitious mine chieftains were Henry Mayer, an outfielder by avocation, and Joe Jones, a pretty fair pitcher who had success in the Reno area with a roundhouse curve ball. He was also a rather silent fellow.

When they arrived at the mining camp, "Lefty" Mayer was assigned a nice comfortable position in the bookkeeper's office, sharpening pencils or something non-arduous. On the other hand, Mr. Jones was assigned a mucker's (shoveling) chore deep in the depths of the mine. After laboring silently underground for several days, he finally blurted: "This job is murder; I don't know how they expect me to pitch Sunday."

Overheard by a miner who was betting his wages on Sunday's game, the remark quickly relayed to the "front office." It developed that the man who had made the original assignment of jobs for the incoming athletes had assumed that any player nicknamed "Lefty" must be a pitcher, and thus would get the cushy job. The situations were hastily reversed, and Mr. Jones rested his arm from then on with no task more strenuous than removing pencil clips or trimming pencils. And the non-pitcher "Lefty" was sent underground.—*May 19, 1971*

Into this Spartan atmosphere came a horde of elite tourists

Colorful characters used to abound in Reno's taverns, before the metropolitan trend of recent years produced a generation of impersonal purveyors. One of the most flamboyant was Bodie Mike. He was strictly out of Damon Runyon, although the Nevada mining camps were a long way from Broadway.

Stumpy, cigar-chompin' and outgoing, he communicated in a rasping, accented voice that he ran saloons, not night clubs. Among his enterprises was at the Depot Bar on Commercial Row where simplicity was emphasized. Shots of booze were poured, draft beer was drawn but a whiskey-water highball was regarded as a fancy mixed drink.

Into this Spartan atmosphere came a horde of elite tourists, taking advantage of a stop by their train at the Reno depot to refresh themselves with their favorite cocktails. A zombie. A daiquiri. A sloe gin fizz. A dry martini. They deluged Bodie Mike with orders for fancy cocktails. He listened with some bewilderment, then growing resentment. Then he exploded.

"Out! Out!" he bellowed at the startled travelers. "To the Riverside!" he pointed doorward. "To the Riverside! This is a saloon!"

—August 10, 1975

The sound of a running motor was like music

The past week's heavy rains in Reno proved one thing—automobiles are still vulnerable to splashes.

Cars go whooshing through deep puddles of rain water, usually without any trouble. But, in spite of modern craftsmanship, some of them are prone to misfortune. Drivers who were making like hydroplanes through the pools suddenly found out their brakes wouldn't work. Other cars simply quit running. Water splashing up into the autos' innards put a damper on the electrical systems.

Every time we see a motorist stranded on a rainy street, we recall a personal, unpleasant incident of 25 years ago. It was during the Truckee River flood of 1950. The river was pouring over its banks, sending a two and three-foot torrent through the adjacent streets, through the main floors and basements of Reno stores and hotels.

Some of the downtown bridges were already closed, when we set out to gather sidelights on the situation. Accompanied by a staff sergeant from Stead Air Base, who was part-timing on the Journal staff, we started our elderly Chevy and roamed the watery streets of Sparks. It was raining hard, just like it did here the other night. We decided to cross the river at the Glendale Bridge, the last crossing at the east end of the valley. The swollen river was not only up to the bridge, but was running across it several inches deep, and climbing rapidly.

It spite of our care, we couldn't avoid creating splashes. The engine went dead. We were stranded in the middle of a bridge covered with rising water. "The distributor got wet," observed the sergeant, helpfully. It seemed like a simple thing to raise the hood, wipe the distributor, cords and spark plugs dry. But when we'd raise the hood (it was the side-lifting kind) to wipe the damp gadgets, the torrent of rain doused them even worse. This was the dilemma, as the river flowing over the bridge was now hub-high.

Finally, the sergeant gallantly stretched his body over the engine and shielded it from the rain while we used handerchiefs, shirt-tails and note paper to wipe the distributor, etc., to a state of dryness. We hastily closed the hood and, drenched and scared, got back inside. Tried the starter. Wouldn't quite catch. The water was now floor-deep. We were just about to abandon the car and try to get out on foot when the starter worked. The sound of a running motor was like music. We inched the car across the rest of the bridge, taking extreme care "not to make waves." And with a new respect for the perils of splashmanship.

—September 14, 1975

Strangers joined hands and snake-danced in long lines through the clubs and streets

"Why don't you write about how New Year's used to be?" suggested a lady of our acquaintance. It's well-meaning ideas like this that shove us further into the Old-Timer category. Like the grizzled (they're always grizzled, never clean-shaven) patriarch saying to the group squatting around the campfire, or the pot-bellied stove in the country store, "Wal, boys, they just don't have New Year's like they used to ... now, back in the winter of '89 ... "

The lady said what she really meant was that we must have had some memorable experiences during our 38 years on the night shift of the Nevada State Journal.

Frankly, since we never kept a scrapbook or notebook, we really can't recall New Year's Eve as amounting to much, memorable-wise. There was always some maneuvering on the part of the staff to get that evening off, or at least, to leave early. But the newspaper had to come out, the presses running at midnight, as they have for more than a century. You just couldn't run it off early and let everyone depart ahead of time. Some crashing local news story was certain to break as soon as the "journalists" departed. For the most part, New Year's Eve has been so dull from a national standpoint that the people manning the UPI and AP bureaus around the country would spend their time composing seasonal greetings on their teletype, in the shape of Christmas trees or bells, etc.

Our personal most exciting New Year's Eve was spent underground in a mine near Silver City, Nev., where rescue crews were attempting to reach miners trapped by a cave-in. We've related this story often, how the paper came out too early on this night to include our rescue story!

Why the rush to get out early? It was the thing to do—get the free paper hats, noise-makers, paper streamers and confetti which were passed out at the downtown clubs. The Bank Club, a huge casino at Center Street and Douglas Alley, where Harrah's Hotel now stands, was the top attraction. Strangers joined hands and "snake-danced" in long lines through the clubs and streets. And, as now, there were many private parties at homes and cafes. Without the grim deterrent of the DUI and other patrols.

Looking further back, it seems that New Year's Eve was more noisy, from a strictly noise standpoint, when we were kids. We kids weren't quite sure of the reason, but we knew it was very important to join in the bedlam. At the stroke of midnight, we'd go outside and beat on tin pans, or blow any kind of horn. The men were blasting their shotguns skyward, and the town siren would wail. Louder explosions could be heard, presumably from dynamite touched off by daring (foolish?) fellows. In the mining towns, Eureka, Tonopah and the others—those mines with steam whistles would sound off. In Sparks, the big steam locomotives of the Southern Pacific shops had been fired up, and their piercing whistles added a (long-departed) sound to the night air's discord. In Virginia City, the youngsters went to the Catholic and Episcopal churches to ring their big bells, pulling on the long ropes until arm-weary.

These noisy customs were carry-overs from the early days of the state. Nineteenth-Century Nevadans were hell on noise, whenever the occasion merited it. They had most of the above-mentioned ear-splitters, plus the town fire bells, cannon salutes or rifle volleys discharged by the militia (National Guard) companies. And blacksmiths' anvils, struck by sledgehammers, gave off loud sounds which could be heard for great distances.

Highlight of the old-time New Year's Day was the custom of calling. Young ladies of the town had previously sent out formal announcements that they would be "at home" on that date. And the young gentlemen of the town, if their hangovers weren't too severe, would dress in their best and make the rounds of the homes. Families also exchanged visits on this day, too. Now we have television's coverage of the parades and football games, preceded the night before by Guy Lombardo.—*December 31, 1975*

An elderly Reno matron leaned over and belted him on the head with her purse

Opening of Reno's baseball season is coming up Thursday night at Moana Stadium, and Dick Green, general manager of the Silver Sox, has given us a flattering invitation to throw out the ceremonial "first ball" of the season.

Guess there isn't much that can go wrong with such a simple feat, except that (1) we may develop arm trouble and fail to produce more than a roller toward the plate; or (2) we might overcompensate and throw the ball over the grandstand.

Things have been known to go wrong with Silver Sox openers before. Something went wrong with the public address system for the very first season opener in 1947 and, as the announcer, we had to inform the fans via an old Navy "blow horn." There were other discomforts in the old ball park, such as dust blowing from the unplanted infield and into the spectators' eyes, and foul tips ripping through the weak chicken-wire in front of the grandstand and bombarding the fans.

There was the time when a gent in the press box, given the signal to start the National Anthem, twice applied the phonograph needle at the wrong speed. The first time the speeded-up tempo sounded like Donald Duck, and the next attempt was slower than molasses in winter.

Newsman Bob Nitsche was Silver Sox business manager for several years. He thought he had all details arranged for his first season opener in Reno. But midway through the game all the lights in the ball park went out. As he groped around in the dark, he encountered one of the club's directors who demanded to know what Nitsche was going to do about it. On another occasion, a light pole caught fire and the game went out in a blaze.

Graduation Day. In June, 1937, I departed from the University of Nevada. As a Senior, I qualified to sit on the Senior Bench.

Most of the incidents occurred at the old (1947-1960) ball park but the new stadium has seen some opening night foulups, too—like the time the color guard and drum corps marched to the outfield to raise the flag, but went to the wrong flagpole where there were no ropes or flag.

Strange and funny things at Moana weren't confined to Opening Night. Each season something happened, particularly at the quaint old park. Some of them involved umpires. One of the first Sunset League umps was on bad terms with Reno fans. The chubby little man refused to keep his car in the parking lot, where it might be molested and he parked it inside the fence down the rightfield foul line. One night he suddenly screamed: "Time!" and scooted down the first base line toward right field. The players and fans were mystified until they learned the ump, Herbie Happ, had spotted some pranksters trying to tip his car over.

Another umpire made a call in the Far West League playoffs which cost Reno the pennant. As he headed for the dressing room, he passed the edge of the third base stands where a dignified and elderly Reno matron leaned over and belted him on the head with her purse.

Umpires often got a vigorous "chewing out" from the late Ray Perry, Reno manager, who also toted a double chaw of chewing tobacco. The Little Buffalo's remarks were accompanied by a spray of tobacco juice, but the worst victim was an ump named Hank Shimada. He was the only one as short of stature as the sawed-off Perry. Thus in their "eye to eye" confrontations, Shimada suffered the full force of Perry's spray.

Freedom of the press came under attack from one umpire. The newsmen, announcer and scorers worked in a small booth built on the edge of the grandstand roof, and it was illuminated only by a single light globe. Some outfielder told the umpire the light bothered him, and the umpire ordered the press box light extinguished. This produced a new crisis—because no one could see his scorebook or notes in the darkness. On came the light, and another ultimatum from the ump, who threatened to forfeit the game to the visitors. We compromised by building a makeshift shade around the light bulb.

There was a tradition of banging out on a press box gong the number of runs scored in each inning. One exuberant young man, after a Reno rally, wielded his hammer so vigorously he also shattered the lone light bulb.

Seldom were umpires actually assaulted but one night a real brawl broke out in front of the umps' room. Finally a husky gentleman from Verdi named Panelli put on his fish and game warden's badge which looked like a policeman's badge, and halted the hostilities.

Covering the games made a long day for the *Gazette* sports reporters who seldom got home before midnight and had to report for work early the next morning. One sports editor, a bachelor, frequently vanished after a few innings, and reappeared later in the game. Bob

Bohon revealed he would leave his wash sloshing around in a laundromat, then had to leave to gather it up.

One of the night owls from the *Gazette* was Rollan Melton, now president of Speidel Newspapers. He not only covered games for the Gazette, but was official scorer, having to immediately mail official forms to the league statistician. Also, he had to telephone the scores to Western Union and Associated Press, all of which meant he was usually the last man out of the park. One such night he not only found himself in darkness, but locked in. Eventually he succeeded in scaling the fence, but not without damage to his clothing which included leaving the seat of his pants on some fencetop splinters.

Not all the funny incidents at Moana, and especially on opening nights, involved non-players. There was one nightmare of an opening inning which all victims will never forget. Glowing reports on a Silver Sox team had come from spring training camp, and fans were already talking of a pennant contender. They swarmed out to opening night in great numbers. The game began with great hopes. It was fine until the first pitch of the first inning, which a Modesto player laced for a triple. Hits, walks and runs followed in dismaying profusion. Reno just couldn't get the side out, until Modesto had scored 10 runs. Ten runs in the top of the first! At that rate, one fan figured, it could be a final score of 90 to 0. Most of the faint-hearted folks went home. How were they to know Reno was going to come back and trim the lead to just one run before the game was over?

A more spectacular event involving animals came during the early days at Moana, when Lou Berrum, ball park owner, kept a small flock of sheep in a pen in left field. He'd let them graze the outfield daytime, easing the grass mowing problem. One night there was a sudden scattering of players and coach from the third base area, as, with a thudding of hooves, the sheep approached at full speed. Someone had opened the gate of their pen, and shooed the sheep toward the grandstand. They stampeded, about four abreast, three rows of them. With two outfielders and the groundskeeper in pursuit, the woolies pounded past the third base bleachers, the Reno dugout and didn't turn until they reached the grandstand behind home plate. Here the herd's compact formation broke up, and they scattered—

"Like a bunch of sheep"—until they were rounded up and taken back to the pen.

The 1976 players are on a spot. How do you follow an act like last year's Silver Sox? All they did, aside from several individual league titles and records, was win both halves of the 1975 schedule and capture the California League pennant. You just don't get Butch Wynegars and Gene Richards every time. Meanwhile, we're just hoping we all get past Opening Night without disaster. —*April 18, 1976*

He'd wait patiently until the expert's headache had cleared and his stomach had settled

When you talk of Nevada journalism, you can run the gamut from Goodman to Higginbotham, throw in Powning and the Sanfords, and many more. But let's not forget that J.H. "Buster" Brown, who worked for the *Journal* 20 years before his retirement in 1957, played a big role in keeping Nevada journalism moving.

He kept the linotypes alive.

Probably no printer in the history of the state knew as much about the inner workings of those huge, complicated machines whose function was to cast solid lines of type from molten lead. It was no easy chore, keeping the linos running. And especially when the *Journal* and *Gazette* used a common print shop with the over-worked machines running continuously from 16 to 20 hours a day. Buster Brown kept his mechanical monsters tuned as finely as a watchmaker regulates a rare timepiece.

This is not to say there weren't other anxieties. Like many printers of that era, Mr. Brown enjoyed a "little nip" now and then. And again. And the linotypes had to limp along in makeshift style until the master machinist got back on the track. The newspaper foremen were remarkably tolerant. Pat Pettipiece once stated that "Buster Brown in his cups is still sharper than any other Fix-It in the state." And he'd wait patiently until the expert's headache had cleared and his stomach had settled. During his periods of transgression, Mr. Brown would hole up next door at Eddie Vacchina's Alpine Bar (now

The Stein). His rambling monologues would denounce various linotype parts salesmen, publishers, printers, and dumb sportswriters who didn't appreciate Canadian hockey.

But about halfway through this career, Mr. Brown suddenly switched habits. He went "on the wagon" as thoroughly as he had been the other way. But his professional skills did not diminish, despite this new-found sobriety. And he not only kept the *Journal-Gazette* machines functioning but he continued to be a savior to country journalism.

We'd see him start out the door, wearing his "traveling" hat and packing his cherished tool box. "Gotta go to Hawthorne," he'd remark, "Jack McCloskey's linotype just broke down." That might be a Wednesday, but the *Mineral County Independent-News* always came out on publication day, Thursday. Or there might be a call for relief from Walter Cox in Yerington, faced with a *Mason Valley News* printing deadline and a dead linotype. Or up to Lovelock, to bail out Paul Gardner and the *Review-Miner*. Or to rescue the Suverkrups in Gardnerville. Hardly a community in western Nevada or eastern California that had a weekly paper failed to benefit by Buster Brown's emergency operations.

And there was little of this stuff of "sending to the factory for parts." Country newspapers couldn't shut down publication to wait. Buster Brown was an expert at give-and-take. Almost every country weekly print shop had a spare, unusable linotype shoved away in a dark corner. If the trouble with the *Tonopah Times-Bonanza's* printing was a broken 3/8 inch frammis-gate, Buster Brown would remember there was one on the old extra machine in Truckee. He'd get a Fallon paper back in business with parts cannibalized from a Portola back shop.

We never did understand how the Reno Newspapers' prize machinist could grab his tool box and go to the rural area, on a moment's notice. But the long-time mechanical superintendent, Vic Anderson, had a rare tolerance in this matter. Vic had been a country paper printer, in Winnemucca and Alturas, himself, and he knew how things were.

Some print shops still have linotypes, but variations of "off-set" printing dominate the industry now. Buster Brown was not entranced with the new paste-up methods, and he was shocked to enter a "composing room" which lacked the clatter, clank and heat of the old linotypes. Nevertheless, up to the last couple of years—he was 87 at his death Wednesday—he was still available for consultation with any of the rural publishers who still use the old methods.

But during his era, the dapper little transplanted Canadian earned his own peculiar niche in Nevada journalism. He kept the linotypes alive. —*November 14, 1976*

The goal of seven daring men was the cargo in the express car

The first great train robbery in the old West took place right here: anyway, right between Reno and Verdi.

On Nov. 5, 1870, the goal of seven daring men was the cargo in the express car of a Central Pacific train from San Francisco. Most lucrative was $30,000 in gold coins, the payroll for the Yellow Jacket mine in Gold Hill. They left their horses in a quarry at Lawton's Springs (now the River Inn) and made their way to the Verdi depot, a few miles west. When the train halted at Verdi, the men boarded it, donned their masks, and soon forced the engineer to stop the train. They ordered him to uncouple the locomotive and express car and, leaving the rest of the train behind, proceeded to the Lawton's quarry. Here the masked men opened the express car at gunpoint, took out the Wells Fargo treasure box and removed $41,000 in gold coins. Then they galloped away. Returning to Verdi, the engineer tried to warn authorities in Reno by telegraph, but the wires had been cut.

However, within four days, all of the bandits were behind bars. Their hurry to spend the loot betrayed them. And $38,000 was recovered. Four of them later escaped prison at Carson but were recaptured.

Ironically, the same train was robbed again, 385 miles away, on the Utah border, 20 hours later! The *Frontier Times* concludes: "It was three years before another man tried his hand at train robbery. The man's name—Jesse James."—*May 29, 1977*

Twelve-mule teams strained to haul heavy machinery to mines

Nevadans, some of them, are commendably active in saluting the past glories of the state. They've paid homage to ghost town sites, long-vanished stagecoach and Pony Express stops, and other trails and places associated with the pioneers.

Now they're going to pay tribute to a dirt road.

This isn't any ordinary dirt road, although it's well over a century old and has been replaced for four decades by a modern concrete highway.

It's the original Geiger Grade, the road that linked Reno and Virginia City since the early 1860s.

Now, hundreds of autos daily whiz up and down State Route 17, most of them carrying tourists drawn by sight-seeing in the old mining camp of the Comstock Lode. And if they see it at all, the motorists don't realize the winding dirt road a half-mile below them once bore heavy traffic, too. Twelve-mule teams straining to haul heavy machinery to mines. Four- and six-horse stage-coaches bringing passengers to and from the bustling silver camp. Single express riders, carrying packets and mail at top speed. Creaking covered wagons toting whole families to a new life on Mount Davidson.

They traveled a winding dirt route surveyed by an engineer named Geiger, whose name the route still honors. There were masked robbers holding up stage coaches, there were hikers who couldn't afford the fare, and there were herds of cattle, sheep and horses being driven to market.

Even the little work locomotives for the construction of the Virginia & Truckee Railroad were literally dragged up the Geiger Grade. It was assumed that when the V&T was completed in the early 1870s, the Geiger Grade would hardly be needed. But traffic merely increased, both on the rail line and the dirt grade which joined the Carson-Reno road at Steamboat Springs.

The advent of the automobile coincided with decline of the railroad, and Tin Lizzies and Flivvers chugged up and down the well-used dirt grade. The V&T directors coppered their bets, however. The railroad operated the auto stage line between Reno and Virginia City and it continued long after the "iron horse" was permanently stabled.

We've had a close personal interest in the old grade, since my father, the late Sen. Will Cobb, drove that auto stage from the mid-1920s for about four decades. Once it had a schedule of two daily round trips, and on peak days, as many as four round trips with passengers and freight. In winters before the highway department had sufficient equipment to keep the grade clear, the V&T stage would do it. Sometimes several huskies from the mining camp would pile into the bus and ride out the road-opening trip. Whenever it got stuck in the drifts, they'd pile out and shovel the path clear. If storms were of such severity as to prevent the bus method, they'd get reinforcements and ride out to the Geiger Grade in the coal truck of fuel dealer Louis Roth. During his years in the state legislature, Will Cobb pressed for a new paved route, and this was accomplished in 1936. The modernized concrete highway followed the same general line of hills and canyons as the old Geiger Grade, but was built several hundred yards higher.

The 41-year-old "new" highway affords some magnificent scenery and, at closer hand, some beautiful trees and brush plus multi-colored rock formations—marred only by weather-worn commercial advertising signs and billboards.

We have a copy of Nevada Highways & Parks, Volume 1, Number 4, which came out in July 1936. It said blasting was necessary along most of the new highway to the 6,000-foot level to attain sufficient width and the necessary six percent grade, or less. The old Geiger Grade had some climbs of 12 percent!

According to the magazine, the cost of the new highway "on the sunset side of the Virginia Range" was only $258,119. It was done by Nevada Highway Department under a Federal Works Program project. A boon to the post-Depression doldrums, the job employed between 300 and 400 workmen "from the labor relief rolls in Reno."

Summarizing benefits of the new route, the magazine editor noted it will provide a high-gear route from Reno to the Comstock Lode … and will help prolong the mechanical life of thousands of motor cars driven over the course.

On Sunday, Aug. 28, a 2 p.m. ceremony will dedicate a plaque honoring the historic old route. Taking part will be Daughters of American Colonist landmarks committee, representatives from state highways and parks departments, plus some "old-timers" of varying vintage from Virginia City who will recall nostalgia associated with the ancient road.

For this writer, it will revive memories of many childhood rides in the old bus, of taking sled rides from summit to bottom of the steep grade, of friends who perished in fatal accidents there, of Double S Bend, Robbers' Roost and Dead Man's Point, of washouts and stuckwheels, boiling radiators, placid porcupines atop nearby trees, and those everlasting putting-on and taking-off tire chains.

—August 14, 1977

The hair-raising dash of one Archie Pearl

In the early days of automobiling, it was an adventure to travel the Geiger Grade, which had a tilt of as much as 12 percent in some places.

One of the most famous rides of this era was recalled last week during dedication of the marker to the old dirt road which carried Reno-Virginia City traffic. Vada Greenhalgh recounted the hair-raising dash of one Archie Pearl, who dealt in scrap iron, junk, draying and hauling.

His old-time truck was loaded high with heavy scrap iron when he set off from Virginia City to Reno. His companion was Charley Ching, a jovial Chinese who operated a cafe on the Comstock.

As soon as they began descent of the steep grade, the laden truck's brakes failed and away they went, gathering speed. With no brakes to slow it, the truck rolled down at an alarming rate. Driver Pearl clung to the big steering wheel and negotiated curve after curve—Dead Man's Point, Double S Bend, Robbers' Roost and the others.

"I kept praying no one was coming up the grade," Pearl said later. By some miracle, no one was coming up the hill, and Pearl's truck careened and lurched through all the hazards until it coasted out on the flat at the bottom of the grade.

Finally, the dazed Chinese passenger spoke. "What the hell's wrong?"

"No brakes," explained driver Pearl, "I got no brakes."

"By golly," observed Charley Ching, "why you no put on some brakes? Better go buy some."

(Mrs. Greenhalgh adds a P.S. to the story. When the travelers got to Reno, Mr. Ching declined to return on Pearl's truck. He bought a ticket on the V&T train.) —*September 4, 1977*

BASQUE CABDRIVER

The August issue of National Geographic *has an excellent article about "Land of the Ancient Basques" and it is preceded by an editor's note: "While the author was gathering material for this article last summer, a Basque cab driver in Biarritz, France, remarked to him with obvious pride: "You know, we have a Basque governor in the United States now."*

"Yes," Mr. Robert Laxalt replied, "he is my brother Paul."
—July 31, 1968

Carano worked 14- to 18-hour shifts learning the baker trade

To be named "Italian of the Year" doesn't necessarily mean the recipient ranks high in old Italy. In fact, he may never have even visited the "Old Country" if the title he receives is in Reno.

For seven years, a number of Reno men of Italian ancestry, and a growing list of guests from California, have been enjoying the "Italian Golf Tournament" here. What with cocktail parties, luncheons, banquets—and golf, too—it's become quite a blowout. And each time an individual is selected for the "Italian of the Year" honor.

This time they feted William Carano, known as Bill to many friends, and as Willie to the real old-time pals. A man who has known plenty of hard work, had a share in building local business, and a role in producing one of Reno's most popular hotels, the Eldorado.

Bill Carano, now 68, was born in Reno. His parents, Ben and Amelia, had immigrated from Italy and the family farm was south of Reno, where Virginia Lake Park is now. When the Caranos gave up the ranch and moved "into town" to High Street, Virginia Lake was just being constructed (circa 1935) and they deeded some of their land to Washoe County for part of the park.

Childhood and youth in Reno was no picnic for Willie Carano, who helped with work on the ranch, later sold newspapers. He got up early to sell *Nevada State Journals* before school ("never was late for class") and after school sold *Reno Evening Gazettes* on the same corners.

His dad worked at the Southern Pacific downtown depot, while Willie Carano attended Northside Junior High. The youngster got a job at the Silver State Bakery, which was in the same block where the Eldorado now stands. He worked long 14 to 18 hour shifts learning the baker trade.

Many old-time Reno families are linked by marriage. Bill Carano married Lena Del Grande; and there were also ties with the Siri clan. The family bought Silver State Bakery (which was later sold to Welsh's Bakery) and the adjacent Reno Hotel. Then William Carano and Lawrence Siri opened, in 1947, Reno Frozen Food Lockers on South Virginia Street, one of the first of its kind in the state. (Later, brother-in-law George Siri bought the operation.)

The next major step for the relatives was the Eldorado Hotel, on North Virginia Street, a project in which all members of the family participated. Bill Carano spends some time daily at the hotel, but he's also engrossed in three hobbies—cooking, gardening and golf. He goes all-out in food preparation for projects of the Elks, Italian Benevolent Society and South Reno Lions. Also, he particularly helps the Lions' broom and light bulb sales to aid the sight-saving program. (His own cooking specialty is ravioli.)

Carano got into golf late in life in an unusual way. His brother-in-law Lino Del Grande, now retired banker, was recovering from a heart attack and taking daily health walks. By coincidence, Lino chose

A fake fight with Bobo Olson, world middleweight boxing champion. I went to San Francisco many times to see him fight.

the back nine of Washoe Course for his afternoon constitutionals, and although he was not yet ready to resume golf, he took along a seven-iron. "Just to swing at the dandelions." On occasions, Willie Carano would accompany Del Grande on the walks and, out of curiosity, took to swinging the extra golf club at a range ball or two, or a ball which Lino just happened to find in his pocket. Carano hit the ball well enough to stimulate him into taking golf lessons from pro Peter Marich. Next step was lessons for his wife, too.

His fraternal groups are grateful for his participation in their projects. They feel the "Italian of the Year" is really a Citizen of the Year.

—September 11, 1977

Unguarded Irishman

The other day a tourist from out of state was wandering down the corridor of Nevada's Capitol building in Carson City. He stopped outside one office, which had a sign identifying it as the governor's office and, since the door was wide open, he stared in. The room was empty except for the big man seated at a desk who gave the visitor a cheery greeting.

"Are you really the governor?" asked the tourist, unable to believe that a state's top office could be that accessible.

"I sure am," responded Mike O'Callaghan, "come on in."

The visitor stepped in gingerly, awe-struck, then asked one question: "Where are all your guards?"

"Oh," airily responded the Guv. "They're probably down the hall drinking coffee, or else sleeping somewhere."

—September 18, 1977

The tension was tightest, the chores seemed impossible

"And there I was, going hand over hand like Tarzan, dangling from that flimsy flume over a pond of quicksand … at 3 o'clock in the morning …"

Fanciful? Seems like. But it relates to what we now consider the worst night of our life—to date.

Did you ever look back over your own life and pinpoint one single day, or night, as the worst you spent? When more unpleasant things happened to you, or the tension was tightest, or the chores seemed impossible? Let's discount personal tragedies, like accidents, etc., and just stick to things like the first day at work on a new job, or a day when everything went wrong.

Our personal "worst" was a night at the "slum pond" of the Arizona-Comstock mill in Virginia City, in the mid-1930s. The Arizona-Comstock had taken over the old-time Hale & Norcross Mine a few blocks below the Fourth Ward School. It built a mill—the shell of which still stands—to work ore. Instead of hauling ore from the mine tunnel of the Norcross, the A-C gouged a huge hole in the side of Mt. Davidson, across the street from, and west of, the Fourth Ward School on "C" Street.

Power shovels loaded big trucks which hauled ore downhill to the mill. Here it went through a rock crusher, a huge revolving tank partly filled with shot-put size iron balls. What with this grinder, running water and chemical treatment, the ore was pulverized into liquid mud. The valuable gold-silver stuff was separated, and the surplus ran out through a small flume to be deposited in the tailings pond, or "slum pond" as it was locally and inelegantly dubbed.

The idea of the tailings pond was to build a huge bank of semivaluable sand to be hauled away and treated at some distant date. The valuable stuff which had been separated in the mill was of more immediate importance, and was prepared for shipment to a smelter.

The word "tailings" has been misapplied to the huge dumps of waste rock seen outside every mine in Nevada. It's common for writers, broadcasters and others, even in tourist guidebooks, to tell the public those big dirt-rock heaps built up laboriously by dumping of countless ore cars, are "tailings." But to a purist, "tailings" mean the residue from mills.

The tailings pond of the Arizona-Comstock, circa 1935-37, was a huge one. It was built by deposits of sandy mud, or muddy sand. This ran in liquid form from the mill via the aforementioned flume. At the pond, the flume forked to right or left, encircling the pond, and one branch of it ran, like a trestle, directly across the pond. The bottom of the flume was perforated with dollar-sized holes, stopped up with tapering wooden plugs.

The idea was to pull out the plugs in a certain area for about 20 feet and let the liquid fall through onto the edges of the pond. If the mixture was thick enough, the sand would be deposited where it fell, and the liquid would run off to a drain in the center of the pond. If the mixture was thin, with too much liquid, the whole thing would run off and would not be saved.

The mixture was governed by a water hose at a point between the mill and the pond. The idea was to keep the mixture thick enough to be deposited, with just enough running water to keep it moving. If the mixture was too thick, it usually jammed and the heavy sand would pack the flume quickly for a distance of several feet. It was the duty of the attendant to clear these jams immediately. It was also his duty to keep building up the banks at the edge of the pond, mucking (shoveling) up the deposited wet sand and tamping it, to build an ever-higher retaining wall.

These were the duties explained to us when we reported for work. We felt fortunate to land this job in those work-scarce post-depression days. We were also familiar with the "horror" stories about the big tailings pond, especially of its semi-liquid center. There was the tale of a worker who, wearing rubber hip boots, had ventured toward that shaky area, and started to sink. Only by dragging himself out of the boots, the legend went, did he save himself. And there was another rumor, which no one really believed, that in a previous year a man's truck had slid into the tailings pond, and when he returned to extricate it—no truck!

Our shift was the "graveyard" one—starting work at 11:30 at night and ending at 7:30 in the morning. Four dollars a day. And no days off.

There were some compensations for this shift. One got to see an occasional movie, or a Sunday ball game; and you could hear the early evening radio shows like Amos 'n Andy. Also, you could see the moon, and watch the dawn. Further, the lights strung around the tailings pond gave an almost festive glow. The light bulbs became encrusted with yellowish mud-spray from the flume, and the effect was unusual.

"By the way," reminded the gentleman of the evening shift, who we relieved, and was giving instructions to the newcomer, "whenever you get all caught up, you should go up to the mill and help 'em fire the ovens." (These were large ovens with bowl-like depressions, used to dry the valuable "concentrates" for shipment. They were heated by burning small logs beneath them.)

Our instructor departed, and we were left alone with the slum pond. Immediately, there was a sound of strung-out splashing. The flume had jammed up and was overflowing for some distance. It wasn't much trouble to clear, and we soon set to work shoveling up the sandy deposits.

Rushing to put the plugs in one area of the flume, and open another section, a chore repeated countless times during the night like a scene from an "I Love Lucy" comedy, got us well saturated. But that was nothing to what happened when the flume across the center of the pond jammed!

There was no way to reach the trouble spot, no firm spot to place a ladder out there in that soggy no-man's land. The only way to get out there was to swing, hand-over-hand. We tried the Tarzan bit. But just before we reached the jam area, the sand had backed up so fast it was right over our head. Thereupon, it spilled over the side. The whole deluge descended on the unfortunate youth—right on the head, then down the neck. We couldn't let go, and drop into that so-called "quicksand" below.

After a desperate struggle, we cleared the sand-jam, swung back to shore and contemplated our fate. That goop from the flume was inside our clothing, from head to foot. Wet and cold, we tried to warm up by starting a wood stove in a little shelter near the pond. It dried the mud, a little. Faced with the prospect of being encased in a mud cocoon, we returned to the tailings pond and began shoveling furiously. How we built those darn banks! Shovel. Tamp. Shovel. Tamp. Run to change the flume plugs. Shovel. Tamp. We hardly noticed the sunrise.

And with the sun, came our relief, the day shift man, George (Shotgun) Dick. He surveyed our night's work with a look which conveyed dismay, disgruntlement and scorn. "Is THAT all you did?" he inquired.

And so ended our first night on the job. —*October 2, 1977*

The sleek Shoshone punched his way through a long string of opponents

It was a modest little obituary, datelined Schurz, Nev., telling of the death there of Ernest Collins, 62. A couple of sentences mentioned his background in boxing. But what memories that little story stirred! Especially for the Nevada fight fans who were around in the late 1930s and saw the sleek Shoshone punch his way through a long string of opponents.

Ernie Collins could punch, he could take a punch, and he was a colorful non-stop action fighter. What they used to call a "club fighter" in those days. He never really reached the big time in boxing, but he was a drawing card in Western arenas.

Born on the Duckwater, Nev., reservation, he was educated at Sherman Indian Institute near Riverside, Calif., where he learned athletics. His family had settled at Schurz, on the Walker Lake Indian Reservation, and, with his brother Frankie, Ernie soon became known around the rural rings of Nevada. Frankie, a lightweight, always trained harder and more seriously. Ernie, a light-heavyweight, was more disdainful of training; he relied on natural ability, stamina and a KO punch to carry him along. (Two years ago he was honorary chairman of the National Indian Amateur Tournament, and in a ringside interview at Stewart, he told Steve Sneddon he always regretted his early indifference to training and temperance.)

Ernie Collins soon established himself as the best in the state at his weight—and above. He fought middles, light-heavies, heavyweights. In Tonopah he stopped towering Edgar Murphy, not quite as fast as Max Baer did. Then Bud Traynor, clever but outweighed Tonopah boxer, led for five rounds, lost in six. "I spent the next week in bed, couldn't get up," recalls Traynor, now a Reno businessman. They thought Ernie was over his head in meeting Tommy Jordan, ringwise veteran heavy, at Tonopah, but he demolished Jordan, cracking the latter's jaw, too. Also came a couple of wins at Fallon over "Kid Gorilla," a massive Indian who bore a striking resemblance to Gardner Allen, giant Golden Gloves amateur heavy champion.

By this time, Ernie was under the wing of George Griffing, suave and enthusiastic Reno businessman who was a one-man manager, second, trainer and press agent. Griffing flooded the West with stories and pictures of his protégé, whom he billed as the "Shoshone Slugger" and then "Reno Ripper" with a deadly "Tomahawk Punch." Collins' best punch was a short overhand right with a cutting effect.

In the late '30s, Collins headlined many Reno cards mainly at the Coconut Grove (a converted dance hall on North Virginia Street, across from what is now Eldorado Hotel). He out-punched the likes of Killer Coates, Pietro Giorgi, Ford Smith, and others. Ernie headlined cards in Oakland, Sacramento, Modesto, Boise, and elsewhere. His arch-foe was Sacramento's Newsboy Millich, who beat Collins in a 10-rounder at Salt Lake City. They also fought in Oakland, and Sacramento's L-Street Arena. After each "road trip," the bubbling manager Griffing would enter our *Journal* newsroom, trailed by the Collins brothers and sometimes Duane Foster, another Schurz heavy, bearing bruises and adhesive strips on their faces, with Griffing brandishing clippings about their fights.

There was no Nevada athletic board then to recognize state champions, but no one disputed Griffing's claim in behalf of Ernie to the heavyweight and light-heavy titles.

Ernie had a few more substantial boosts, however. In 1937 *Ring Magazine* selected him as the Outstanding Prospect in the world, in his division. And he fought for the American Indian heavyweight championship, narrowly losing a 15-round decision to nationally-regarded Junior Munsell, right in the big Chickasaw's home town of Ponca City, Okla. And Ernie got a brief fling "Back East." He was sent back for handling under an Eastern manager, who changed his style and his name but didn't get him much action.

We were surprised one day to get a letter from New Jersey with the return address topped by "Chief Red Bull." The Eastern handlers didn't think "Ernie Collins" sounded Indian enough for the press, so they gave him the "Red Bull" handle. He trained with stablemate Lee Savold, who got an unsuccessful crack at Joe Louis, but "Red Bull" Collins only had a few bouts around New York City and environs. Chafing under the inactivity, and homesick for the Nevada reservation, he came home. World War II had broken out, he enlisted and served in the Army, and that was the end of his ring career.

Last time we heard from Ernie, he telephoned from Stillwater (Fallon) to tell of the death of his brother Frankie. That was a couple of years ago. Now, the saga of the fighting Collins brothers has closed, except when old-timers talk with awe of those rip-roaring ring rousers of four decades back. —*June 18, 1978*

The famous old battleship was plowing its way into the South Pacific

Among the many who attended the Fausto (Foe) Mentaberry retirement party in Reno the other night was his brother Henry Mentaberry of Winnemucca. There were many old acquaintances who hadn't seen each other in years and years, and conversations turned to "small world" reunion anecdotes.

Hank Mentaberry recalled his, aboard the USS Nevada during the late part of World War II. The famous old battleship which bore this state's name was plowing its way into the South Pacific.

"Between the crew and the soldiers it was transporting, there must have been 5,000 aboard. One day, to pass the time, they started wondering where the different guys came from. The M.C. would shout: 'Anyone here from Texas?' and a couple hundred fellows would cheer and wave."

"'Who's from California?' and another bunch would respond."

"Finally the guy hollered, 'Well, this is the USS Nevada. Anyone here from Nevada?' There was a silence and then a big groan when I finally stood up—the only Nevada man among those 5,000 fellows on the ship Nevada."

"'Throw him overboard!' they all hollered."—*September 3, 1978*

All sorts of schemes were presented, including various ideas on how to tap mighty Lake Tahoe

Atop Lakeview Hill, where Highway 395 starts its descent into Carson City, or into Washoe Valley if you're heading toward Reno, stands an old-fashioned house. Hundreds of motorists pass it every day, without a glance or thought concerning the building on the west side. It's more than a century old, and although the thousands of travelers who have whizzed past it over the years do not realize it, the elderly house is the last visible relic of one of the greatest engineering feats of the 19th century.

This old house is not run-down or dilapidated because it has been in continual use for 105 years. It's in use as the home of the state watermaster, and headquarters for the Marlette Water System.

In the earliest days, the 1860s, the site accommodated a stage-coach stop. Then it was the site of the Thompson Inn. This hostelry burned down in 1871, and was not rebuilt. However, it was succeeded by the present structure as a home for various officials and caretakers of the water system.

AA

Just learned that in a certain central Nevada town, where facilities for meetings are limited, the AA (Alcoholics Anonymous) group holds Sunday night meetings in a building which houses the town's best-known bar.
—January 21, 1979

The importance of the ancient house which stands next to the entrance of the prestigious Lakeview Estates development has not been lost by those Nevadans striving to maintain recognition of the state's past. Earlier this year, it was officially entered into the National Register of Historic Places. The action was announced by the Historic Preservation officer, Kimberly Wood, who said the structure would be eligible for federal preservation grants.

While the present water works is called the Marlette system, it was better known in previous years as the Virginia & Gold Hill Water Co.

It began during the boom days of the Comstock Lode. For the first decade of mining in the Virginia City area, water was sufficient. It came from wells, springs and tunnels on Mount Davidson. But as deep mining progressed, these sources dried up. There was not enough water to serve thriving communities totaling 30,000 persons, as well as the machinery of the huge mines and mills. All sorts of schemes were presented, including various ideas on how to tap mighty Lake Tahoe.

The best solution, however, lay in a sizable, isolated lake high in the mountains above Lake Tahoe. This was Marlette Lake. The big problem was: Marlette rested at the lofty altitude of 7,833 feet and Virginia City's was 6,535. The two points were on separate mountain ranges, with a deep valley between them. It was a staggering problem, but not one to daunt the daring engineering minds of the 1870s.

They conceived a great "inverted siphon," a pipeline which would carry the water down one mountain from Marlette and across a broad valley, then up a steep mountain to the Comstock Lode cities!

The waters of Marlette were conveyed by a wooden flume, with use of Hobart Creek, to the top of a huge pipeline. This plunged down the mountain, a drop of 1,997 feet to the floor of Washoe Valley, which it entered where the Lakeview Hill house now stands.

The tremendous pressure from this sheer plunge forced the water through the pipe across Washoe Valley and up the flank of the big mountain to the east. Here the siphon emptied its liquids into a big holding pond, the Five Mile Reservoir (altitude 6,645 feet). From here, it was conveyed by wooden flume—20 inches wide and 18 inches deep, to the cities of Virginia and Gold Hill. Its actual length reached six miles to a point above the north end of Virginia City. It emptied into wooden storage tanks above the towns, as well as into a big holding pond called the Divide Reservoir. This was on the ridge above Gold Hill.

Construction of the water system was a marvel in daring, skill and speed. In 1871, control of the Virginia & Gold Hill Water Co. passed from the hands of banker William Sharon into those of John Mackay, James Fair and associates—soon to be known as the "Bonanza Kings."

With their financing and drive, the project moved at top speed, following the directions of engineer Hermann Schussler.

The best of iron was imported from Scotland, in the form of iron plates which were then shaped at a San Francisco foundry. The pipe sections were "tailored" to fit the shape of certain curves along the route. The pipe was tested at the foundry at a maximum pressure of 1,400 pounds per square inch.

Details of the spectacular project can be found in Hugh Shamberger's "Water Supply for the Comstock," one of several booklets he has authored on historic mining camps of Nevada. His excellent research describes the arrival of the first Marlette water. Newspapers of August 3, 1873 reported the jubilation of the inhabitants of the parched mining camps. About 13,000 people gathered to see the historic debut of the water from the distant Sierra Nevada lake. Others celebrated it with cannon shots, rockets and bonfires which blazed all day and night.

(This columnist's own grandmother told us of seeing that event. Jeanette Simpson Harris was a child of eight when her parents took her to the reservoir to see the water arrive. "It was awfully muddy for hours," she recalled, "but everyone was nearly crazy with joy.")

Three different pipelines were laid over the same route. In the 1950s, some of the original pipe was used to replace the wooden flume from Five Mile Reservoir to the Virginia City tanks. But the old 18x20-inch wooden flume will be recalled with affection by many a Comstocker. The natives were proud of their sweet and pure drinking water, although there were some times when the quality fell—such as lizard, skunks or other critters falling through loose boards and affecting the flavor. Herds of sheep crossing Mount Davidson often damaged the flume, too.

(And some of the water at the end of the flume found its way into a boy-constructed dam in Byrnes Ravine. Somehow, mysterious holes or loose boards in the flume leaked out enough water to stock a "swimming pool" which could be better described as a muddy wallow known as Byrnes' Pond.)

Water stored in the tanks above Virginia City was so high above the town that it generated terrific pressure. When fires broke out in the town, the water pressure required two or three men to man the writhing hoses with the old-fashioned nozzles.

Shamberger reports the water system totaled 20 miles in length at its peak, and its maximum capacity was 10 million gallons delivered daily in 1882.

The water company had its own telephone system so that attendants at various stations could keep in touch with each other and headquarters in Virginia City and Lakeview House. The system was operated by James Leonard from 1906 to 1959, and then by his son Hobart. "The main task of the Virginia Water Co.," observes author

Shamberger, "was to keep the system in operating condition, which at times during winter weather was a task of considerable magnitude."

In anticipation of receiving a rich government contract for a missile site, the Curtis Wright Co. bought up most of Storey County's land in the 1950s, including the water system. This didn't materialize, however, and most of the holdings were disposed of. The State of Nevada and Carson City acquired most of the Marlette Water System in the early 1960s, as a source of Carson water supply. Storey County now operates its own section of the system into Virginia City.

And the 105-year-old house at Lakeview continues to be the focal point of one of the greatest engineering feats in modern history. It deserves its new status as a historical landmark.

—September 24, 1978

Big-name bands provided music, and stars of show biz entertained the dinner and cocktail crowds

The "Grand Old Dame" of Nevada hotels had a birthday last week. Now 31 years old is hardly enough to label a woman a "Grand Old Lady," but when it comes to hotels in the state of Nevada, it's a different perspective.

True, there are older hostelries than the Mapes Hotel in Reno—the Riverside and El Cortez among them—and older ones in the rural towns, which date back well into the 19th century. But for sheer beauty of architecture, and community and social service, the handsome structure at First and Virginia streets in Reno deserves its matriarchal title.

The hotel stands on the site of what was previously the Reno post office, an imposing structure with stone steps and columns. And in turn, it had stood on the site of a hay and grain store co-owned by George W. Mapes, a contemporary of Reno founder Myron Lake, and grandfather of Gloria and Charles Mapes.

It was on Dec. 17, 1947 that the Mapes Hotel opened its doors. It made an impact on the life of Reno, a relief after the drab stalemate of the war years.

The Mapes family—Charles W., his sister Gloria and their late mother—put together the plans which were culminated on that date in 1947. Reno responded with zest. Official "counters" at each door checked off a total of 20,000 visitors that first day! They were eager to see the hotel with such superlatives as: First high-rise in Nevada; First major air-conditioned building in the state; Largest apartment house (there were 40 housekeeping suites); Most elevators—four. Up to then no building had more than two lifts. It was the tallest building in the state—12 floors, about 150 feet.

Crowning glory of the new hotel was the Sky Room, on the 12th floor, with a view of the Truckee Meadows. Here, big-name bands provided music, and stars of show biz entertained the dinner and cocktail crowds.

From windows of the lofty Sky Room, patrons could look out on the lights and rooftops of Reno's downtown buildings, and see the Sierra Nevada in the distance. This was Reno's version of San Francisco's Top of the Mark, and it was twice as high as the previous tallest building (El Cortez with six floors). Newer structures such as First National Bank, Harrah's and MGM have now surpassed the Mapes in height, but the view remains superb.

The Sky Room was an instant success. The four elevators from the lobby were busy hoisting customers to the 12th floor to hear the house band, Joe Reichman's orchestra. It was followed, over the years, by such resident bands as Henry King's and Leighton Noble's.

"Me and My Shadow" was heard twice nightly when Ted Lewis opened the first floor show atop the Mapes.

The years of the Sky Room are steeped in nostalgia as the famous entertainers are recalled. There was Milton Berle telling jokes, the Andrews Sisters with their WW II rhythm, Sammy Davis dancing away, ventriloquist Edgar Bergen and his Charlie McCarthy rousting each other, the piano magic of Liberace, the dry humor of George Gobel, the zany antics of the Marx Brothers.

Biggest draw of all, however, was the sexpot trio—Lily St. Cyr, Gypsy Rose Lee and Mae West in one unbelievable threesome. "They packed in the biggest crowds in Sky Room history," Charles Mapes recalls.

A big favorite was Reno-based Beatrice Kay, the "Gay Nineties Girl," and there was operatic singer Helen Traubel.

Want some real nostalgia? Just think of the pre-inflation salaries these big-name entertainers, among the world's greatest stars, were paid. The Will Mastin Trio—Sammy Davis, Jr., his father and uncle— earned a combined $350 a week! But in 1960, during the Olympics, Sammy Davis was paid $17,000 a week. What would he command today? And a piano player named Liberace took down $250 a week, Ann-Margret earned $250, while comedian Gobel topped them with $500 per.

In its three decades existence, the Mapes Hotel has had some illustrious moments and some harrowing ones.

In the latter category were two of Reno's major floods, 1950 and 1955 when the rain-swollen Truckee River next door overflowed its banks into downtown streets. Water was rushing three or four feet deep down First Street.

"We kept it out of our main floor by sandbagging the doors," Charles Mapes recalls, "but a wall at the alley (Truckee River Lane) gave way and the flood poured into our basement."

That brought about the most chilling experience in the life of the Reno-born ex-racing boat driver and big game hunter. "I was down in the basement to help clear out our staff. The water was four feet deep and rising fast. I had two of the maids perched on my shoulders and was trying to get out. Fortunately, I got to the steps by the barber shop and got out a few seconds before the basement filled to the ceiling!"

Five years later, during the 1955 flood, Mapes had another narrow escape. He was in front of the hotel supervising rigging of a line to an across-the-street building so that hot coffee and food could be ferried to isolated hotel guests. A torrent of flood water carried the hotel man down First Street where he clung to a parking meter. "Luckily, the National Guardsmen were across the street at the City Hall and they crossed the street in an amphib vehicle and grabbed me."

Among the brighter spots in the Mapes nostalgia book was the 1960 Winter Olympic Games, when the hotel provided headquarters for U.S. and foreign newsmen for an International Press Club. It was also an unofficial headquarters for Olympic officials, coaches, athletes and spectators who used Reno as a gateway to Squaw Valley.

The hotel has also been headquarters for innumerable civic events, and Mapes is proudest of the benefit held there for victims of the Lake Street fire. "More than $50,000 was raised for those people," Mapes recounts. "Harold Smith and Ed Sahati got into a bidding contest during the auction and a child's tricycle went for $17,000."

The hotel had its share of celebrities—Marilyn Monroe and Clark Gable during filming of "The Misfits"; assorted Rockefellers—Nelson, Winthrop and Bobo; and A.P. Gianinni, financial wizard who founded Bank of America. Labor figure Harry Bridges was married there. And so was Del Webb, the baseball-construction giant who wed and honeymooned at the Mapes. —*December 24, 1978*

Sinatra's torrent of vituperative language sizzled the phone lines

The death of ex-newsman and gambling control chief Ed Olsen stirred memories for many Nevadans.

Perhaps the best-known anecdote has already been related—when he blew the whistle on Frank Sinatra and revoked the singer's Nevada gaming license. Sinatra, as part owner of a Lake Tahoe casino, had been warned about association with notorious underworld figures. When he ignored the state agency's messages, and entertained a Chicago figure who was a no-no in Nevada's "black book," Sinatra was punished promptly.

Stunned and infuriated, Sinatra called Olsen personally and unleashed a torrent of vituperative language which must have sizzled the phone lines. The patient Olsen weathered the storm of abuse and informed Ol' Blue Eyes that the revocation remained.

—*January 14, 1979*

It was the most notorious divorce case of the century

Obituaries carried by the wire services about the beloved movie actress of yesteryear, Mary Pickford, didn't mention Nevada's most famous divorce case. "America's Sweetheart" died this week at age 86.

She was survived by her husband of 40 years, Buddy Rogers, who was preceded by Douglas Fairbanks, Sr. However, to marry the dashing Fairbanks, she divorced another movie star, Owen Moore, in Nevada 59 years ago.

It was the most notorious divorce case of the century, before "Reno divorces" became commonplace, especially in the 1920s and '30s. The state's divorce laws then were more liberal than other states', but not as easy as they were later made.

In 1920, there were several routes for marital breakups, involving residence of one or both parties in various counties, etc. The residence period was six months. Mary Pickford took up residence in Douglas County, on a ranch near Minden, on Feb. 15, 1920. She hired a young Reno attorney, Pat McCarran, later to become a prominent U.S. Senator.

About three months later, Owen Moore showed up in Minden with a party of photographers, "for the purpose of taking mining pictures." At the Minden Inn, he was served with a summons.

Eventually, the case came to court before Judge Frank P. Langan. The court was satisfied the parties had acted in good faith, that Mary had come to Douglas County for her health.

The presence of the husband saved her many more months' residence, according to a loophole in the law. The judge was satisfied with Moore's explanation he had come to Nevada to "look for a coal mine"—a technicality which at the judge's suggestion, was changed to a "gold mine" at Virginia City.

The decree of divorce was granted, but the affair wasn't settled. There was a public outcry, including criticism from the Nevada State Federation of Women's Clubs. And Attorney General Leonard Fowler attacked the decree, hinting darkly of "collusion."

However, the divorce held up. Owen Moore went back to Hollywood, without discovering his coal-gold mine; and Mary Pickford, her health remarkably improved by her stay in Nevada's good air, also returned to the film capital to marry the handsome and adventurous Douglas Fairbanks.

She had also spent some time in Reno. Some time later, her attorney, Pat McCarran, acquired the stately mansion at the northwest corner of Court and Arlington (then Belmont) streets. The popular rumor was that Miss Pickford had purchased the mansion and presented it to attorney Pat as a gift. This report has been vigorously denied, throughout the years, by members of the late senator's family.

—*June 3, 1979*

The Northern Saloon and Casino
flourished as Tex Rickard put Goldfield on the map

You see, Tex Rickard was the most colorful, famous and successful fight promoter of his time—1906 to 1924—and perhaps of all time. And he got his career start in Nevada.

Tex Rickard was a teenage cowboy in Texas. Then, when news of the Klondike gold rush swept the world in the late 1890s, he joined the trek to Alaska and Canada. Before sinking a pick in the dirt of the Yukon, he learned that extracting gold from miners over the poker, roulette and blackjack tables was less arduous than digging it out.

He took his new-found knowledge of gambling to another mining boom camp—Goldfield. There his Northern Saloon and Casino flourished, and Rickard put Goldfield on the map in a manner different from the silver seekers. He promoted a world championship fight between lightweights Battling Nelson and Joe Gans. That was in 1906. He also staged more obscure Goldfield-Tonopah bouts featuring a young Jack Dempsey.

Four years later Rickard persuaded big Jim Jeffries, who had retired undefeated as world heavyweight champion in 1905, to come out of seclusion and try to regain his crown from the title holder, Jack Johnson. Great public pressure literally forced the stolid Jeff to "come back." So did a $75,000 bonus from Rickard, just for signing the contract.

Rickard first scheduled the fight in San Francisco, but the governor of California nixed the affair. So it was hastily removed to Reno, after friendly approval from Governor Denver Dickerson's administration.

The cowboy-hatted Rickard had a promoter partner, John J. Gleason, of whom little is known. They shared a $120,215 payoff from movie rights. The gate admission ($50 tops) amounted to $270,775. Johnson's winner's share of the $100,000 purse was $60,000 and loser Jeffries' was $40,000. The fighters had also received large bonuses from Rickard for signing, so there was little left for the promoters after paying expenses. (No tax was paid, however.) Official attendance was 15,760 paid, while a large number "sneaked in" and it is estimated that 20,000 were actually in the Reno arena. (The 15,760 figure remained the largest attendance for any event in Nevada until two years ago when UNR Wolf Pack played UNLV Rebels in a Las Vegas football game.)

(The partners also escaped the fee for a referee. Rickard himself served as the "third man" in the ring, a job which ended in the 15th round with the dazed Jeffries slumped on the canvas.)

Successful Tex Rickard went back East and became matchmaker for Madison Square Garden, also promoting some outdoor classics including the first million-dollar gate, the Dempsey-Carpentier fight. Reunited with Dempsey, whom he had helped get a start years before in Nevada mining camps, the Texas Cowboy promoted most of Dempsey's early big fights. There was Dempsey-Willard, and Dempsey-Firpo, also Tunney-Greb and many others.

His untimely death in 1924 ended a promotional career which started in Nevada and culminated in New York. —*June, 1979*

My God, Walter, what have you sent us into?

What was your first impression of Nevada? Do you remember where it was and how it looked when you got your first glimpse of the state?

This query does not include the initial look by native Nevadans, who are now considerably outnumbered by residents who came here from other climes.

Was it at the state border near Verdi, if you drove in from California, or at Topaz if you motored up from Southern California? Or at the Reno or Las Vegas airports, the Utah line at Wendover, or the highways from Idaho or Oregon?

Regardless of the memories of our readers of their first impression of Nevada, we are sure they won't compare with that of a cultured, apprehensive lady from the East, 62 years ago.

The arrival of Euphenia Clark. She was the wife of Walter E. Clark, who had been chairman of the political science department at City College of New York.

Euphenia Clark had led a rather sheltered life, confined to New England and Manhattan Island, the heart of New York City. She was well-educated and cultured, with a talent for music. It was a long way from the music salons of Manhattan to Reno, where her husband had just been appointed president of University of Nevada.

Mrs. Clark went West ahead of her husband, who remained behind to complete his semester at CCNY, to establish their new home in the president's house on the Reno campus. On that train trip across the country she was accompanied by the four children—Walter Van Tilberg Clark, who was to become Nevada's most famous author; another son, Dave Clark; daughter, Euphenia M., who would become Mrs. Jim Santini, Sr. (mother of the current congressman); and daughter Miriam, who later would wed John Chism (of the ice cream family and later mayor of Reno).

The transcontinental train trip would take the erstwhile Manhattan family through varied scenery—over great rivers, through big cities, broad wheat fields, wooded mountains. But nothing to prepare them for the first sight of their new state.

Mrs. Clark awakened early on the final day of the journey. She was aroused by the train stopping. Putting her head through the curtains of the berth, she asked a porter where they were. "It's Nevada, lady. We're in Nevada."

Excitedly, Mrs. Clark dressed in a hurry. She was eager for a first glimpse of the state for which they had departed the skyscrapers of Manhattan. Would it be a gentle forest, rippling streams or lush green fields?

She rushed to the observation platform, took one horrified look and screamed. And screamed. "My God, Walter," she denounced her husband, 3,000 miles back on the East Coast, "What have you sent us into?"

For some reason, the train had stopped at the Humboldt Sink. This was where remnants of the little Humboldt River ended in the desert, spreading across alkali flats, and vanishing. As far as the shocked newcomer could see was a desolate vista. No trees. No farms. No grass. No sparkling streams. Even the moon's surface, as conceived by scientists, looked better. Stunned, Euphenia Clark returned to her compartment, and wept. This was to be her new home? Nevada?

It wasn't until a few hours later that the train pulled into the depot of Reno, and she saw a pretty little city with handsome houses, a glittering river and trees everywhere. She quickly loved the new home on the charming little university campus and took an active role in Reno's modest social and cultural life. It was a pretty nice place, after all, and she lived the rest of her life here, content.

But she always recalled, with a laugh, that horrifying moment back in 1917 when she got her first glimpse of Nevada. —*July 8, 1979*

The Falstaffian character was one of boxing's most colorful characters

The wire services' stories emphasized the night Tony Galento *almost* became world heavyweight champion, in their accounts of the death of "Two Ton" last Sunday. Correctly so, because the short fat man from New Jersey came close to dethroning invincible Joe Louis.

However, we had other thoughts about the Falstaffian character who was one of boxing's most colorful, and crude, characters.

We thought back to the time when, 40 years ago, a few months before he fought Joe Louis, Galento had an escapade in Reno. He was touring the country, picking up paydays for exhibitions, and enthralling the local press everywhere with profane and bigoted statements about the champion, the most printable being the off-quoted: *"I'll moider da bum!"*

He came into Reno one day early 1939, signed by promoter Harry Myerfield for a four-rounder in the Olympic, a compact-sized arena on East Plaza Street.

Galento did not excite the blasé Reno fans because prices had been raised to see him in a workout with a sparring partner. The element was curiosity because Galento was the most controversial and colorful ring character of his time. He was even in the comic pages. The short, burly, ornery Ruffy Balenki in the Joe Palooka strip was obviously a Galento prototype.

We visited Tony on the afternoon of his Reno bout. A fledgling sportswriter, we were awed at the sight of Galento and his dour manager, Joe Jacobs, puffing big cigars and quaffing tall highballs. Timidly, we asked him about his reputed beer guzzling capacity. "Never touch the stuff," he proclaimed, "on the day of a fight," he qualified. "Wait'll tonight." And he downed another Bourbon.

The 5-foot-9 Galento must have weighed more than 250 when he climbed through the ropes, with some difficulty, that night. For four uneventful rounds he puffed and ponderously swung at the wary sparmate. Reno fans were unimpressed. "Louis will punch holes in him," they agreed.

Later that night Galento made the rounds of downtown Reno. He was surrounded by curious fans in the Bank Club on Center Street, then the state's biggest casino. Behind the long bar there was a fishbowl-sized goblet. It had a placard: *"Reserved for Two-Ton Tony."* That night it was filled with beer and Galento posed with it. We still have that picture. Then he guzzled the whole thing!

"I'll moider da ——," he announced to the cheering throng.

Later he informed us he was hungry for Chinese food, and we steered him to the nearby Dog House, where Mr. Gee concocted Oriental tasties. He shoveled down the food as fast as the waiters brought it. He and Jacobs found their way to the dice table, and this writer, a weary and satiated companion by this time, slipped out the door.

In fact, the *Journal* office was right next door to the Dog House. Next afternoon, while tapping away at our typer, we were startled by a visitor. "Where's that fat ——?" growled cowboy-hatted Al Hoffman,

With my bride, Olga Glusovich.

owner of the night club. "What train did he take? I'll get an airplane and track him down!"

The raspy-voiced Hoffman asserted that Galento and Jacobs owed him a grand and he was going to pursue them to the ends of the earth to recover it. He claimed that sometime around 4 or 5 a.m., they were "in" for about a thousand dollars. When an accounting was suggested, Hoffman claimed, the pair said their $1,000 for the exhibition bout had been stowed in the El Cortez safe, and that they'd go right over and get it.

"They never came back," snarled Mr. Hoffman. "They hopped the next train East. I don't know which train, however. But if I find out, I'll fly back there and make 'em pay up."

Galento would knock him through the roof, we cautioned.

"Oh, no," asserted the casino chief, displaying his .38 pistol.

We never heard if Mr. Hoffman carried out his threat.

Three months later Galento climbed into the ring against the awesome Brown Bomber, a grotesque figure against the sleek champion. He held his own for two rounds, then electrified the 35,000 fans by blasting Louis to the canvas with a sweeping left hook. That was his moment of glory. Louis arose and punched him out in the next round.

About half a dozen years ago, Galento re-visited Reno. He came here with other big names of the past to attend the Golden Age of Boxing reunion in the Mapes Skyroom. He seemed much older and smaller—more quiet and modest, too. No longer the loud and foulmouthed braggart of that 1939 escapade. Illness, and time, had changed him. He only reacted with a half-smile when presented that picture taken in Reno in 1939 when he had hoisted, and gulped down, the fishbowl-sized goblet of beer *"Reserved for Two Ton Tony."*

—July 25, 1979

Elsie burst on the scene like a bombshell, high-stepping, and strutting

They played the first night football in Nevada.

They could be called Nevada's first professional team—sort of.

They had the nation's most famous mascot, with the prettiest knees.

They had one of the most colorful nicknames—"Eleven Old Men."

They played 40 years ago and have decided it's time for a reunion.

Looking over a long list of athletes who played with the Reno Townies in the late 1930s and into the '40s, and noting that quite a number of them are deceased, Lou Spitz remarked, "We decided we'd better not wait for the 50th to hold a reunion."

Actually, the time and place for a gathering of the "Eleven Old Men" alumni are not definite, but will probably be in the form of a Reno luncheon sometime soon. That session should revive many tall tales of the tribulations and wanderings of the Reno Athletic Club.

It was formed in late 1938. The first game was at the old Reno High School field on East Ninth Street (where the Washoe School administrative buildings now stand), and the Townies used uniforms borrowed from Reno High. Bill Nash, ex-Pennsylvania end and a Reno radio announcer, had been critical of the university team. He was challenged to "show us how to play." Nash suited up, and in the last minute of the game, caught the winning TD pass from Bud Beasley.

Lou Spitz, tackle, and Al Lansdon, center, were the co-coaches and managers of the Townies during their four-year existence. During that era, they played Lassen Junior College of Susanville several times, also the Sacramento, Martinez, and Antioch teams, the Ely Alleycats, Fresno Crushers, and the Butte (Montana) A.C. There was also a rival local team, sometimes called Reno Merchants and/or Gateway A.C. After playing each other, they merged forces.

The nickname was a play on that hung on the U.S. Supreme Court— "Nine Old Men"—by President Roosevelt.

Sharing public interest was the team's mascot, Miss Elsie Crabtree. As a majorette at Nevada, she wowed the conservative campus. Majorettes and cheer leaders had been undistinguished by their modest, sometimes drab outfits and maneuvers. Elsie burst on the scene like a bombshell. High-stepping, strutting, she wore a brilliant costume which included shiny shorts and a mid-thigh skirt. Her high-kicking style awakened the fans and students. But the excitement was quenched when the very conservative dean of women issued an order that Elsie must revert to a sub-knee-length skirt (and panties of the same color) and cease exposing her knees.

Elsie rebelled and her stubbornness was supported by the press and fans. The dean of women won the battle but Elsie won the war. The publicity brought her fame, and lucrative offers for appearances. She was invited to lead the noted Hollywood Christmas parade. Reno was plastered with stickers: "We Want to See Elsie's Knees."

The "Eleven Old Men" adopted Elsie as their mascot and she gave halftime exhibitions at Fallon, Ely and Butte, among others. She got a $1,000 guarantee to appear in Butte, almost double what the Reno football team got for playing there. "We had to borrow Elsie's $1,000 to get home," recalls Spitz.

Our earlier remark about the "first professional team" was a jest. Financing was nil, and so were gate receipts. Bill Thomas recalled his share after one game was 75 cents, and it cost him $35 to have a broken wrist fixed.

At one Thanksgiving Day game in Ely, the modest advance guarantee melted away on the previous evening of festivity. Thus there was nothing left to pay the hotel bill, much less a Thanksgiving dinner. It was discovered Bud Beasley had the only checkbook in custody. "Hey, Bud, you take care of this now, like a good fellow, and we'll all pay you back when we get to Reno." That was the approach used to separate the halfback-teacher from his funds. We doubt if Bud has ever been recompensed, even 40 years later.

Some of the Townies' plays were very original, and bordered on the daffy. They even had majorette Elsie Crabtree in a couple of games for a fake field goal try. Probably the most spectacular play executed by the "Eleven Old Men" was a pass hurled by Alf Sorensen which sailed 55 yards through the air to end Joe Cleary.

They pioneered night football in Nevada, at least in Northern Nevada. (Someone said a nocturnal game was played in Boulder City previously.) They played Lassen J.C. under the baseball arcs at Moana Park on Sept. 27, 1940. In spite of George Solari's plunging for Reno, the Townies fell before the triple threat skill of Susanville's dashing little Johnny Evans.

The games were spirited, especially against the Sacramento Wildcats. Wolf Pack star Marion Motley was the referee, and he was kept busy breaking up fights. "I came as a football referee, not a boxing referee," he complained.

Sometimes the traveling squad was as scanty as only 16 players, and once, at Susanville, the Old Men had just one substitute—Walter Baring, who later became a U.S. Congressman. In this game the team had only 11 pairs of football shoes, and every time there was a substitution, there was a time out while shoes were exchanged.

The upcoming reunion is actually not the first for the "Eleven Old Men." In 1966 they held a Reno luncheon in honor of a visit by Elsie Crabtree Evans. They put up a big banner at the Sky Room: "Welcome Home, Elsie the Knees."

Incidentally, Elsie, although long since married and a mother, went on to get her diploma in engineering. She is now the assistant city engineer in Tucson, Ariz.

Advent of World War II put a finish to the town team. Many of them entered the armed services and wartime conditions ended any further activity. Here is a list of, as far as we can gather, men who played for the "Eleven Old Men": Gino Quilici, Alf Sorensen, Dick Taylor, Walt Powers, Gordon Garrett, Bud Beasley, Joe Cleary, Bill Nash, Kevin Callahan, Don Zunnini, Hollis McKinnon, Harry Bradley, Jack Horgan, George Solari, Ted Demosthenes, Elmer Ihrig, C.J. McEwan, John Gustafson, Jim McDonald, Joe McDonald, Bob McDonald, Johnny Brucker, Pete Linson, Bob Erickson, Lou Spitz, Joe Lommori, Al Lansdon, Vic Becaas, Jim Shepley, Bill Thomas, Harry Mornston, George Koocher, Bob Cash, Dale Hansen, Jay Lockridge, Jerry Dellanoy, Boke Robinson, Dave Morman, Elmer Ihrig, Bull Harrigan, Gill Depoali, Howard Guinn, Joe Kievett, Cod Alexander, Lefty Mayer, Van Zant, Bing Avansino, Walt Baring, Al Talcott, Harley Leavitt, Sam Drakulich, Jim Underhill, Fred Galloway, and Dave Clark. —*December 30, 1979*

I got my foot in the stirrup and was immediately bucked off

What small boy hasn't longed, wistfully, for a Shetland Pony? Well, I have, and my wish was fulfilled. And I tell you, it ain't that great!

As a small boy in Virginia City, I was convalescing from a serious illness. My parents saw me looking at the catalog which depicted the "genuine cowboy suits" which were popular in the early 1920s. It consisted of a so-called cowboy hat, with a flat brim; a bandanna neckerchief and simulated chaps of artificial leather with some kind of tin bangles on the legs. They sent for this outfit, but something was lacking: a horse.

My father saw an ad in a San Francisco newspaper about a sale of Shetlands. My parents thought having a pony would be a good way to help me recover from the heavy illness. So we all started off for San Francisco in my dad's truck.

In San Francisco, the diminutive animals trotted dutifully around a corral. One, somewhat larger than the others, was offered at a bargain price. At that time, we didn't know why it was a bargain.

I had day dreams of riding in the back of the truck with my new animal pal. But it didn't come out that way. The pony was a bit reluctant to go up a ramp and into the truck. He's a little nervous, explained the salesman, as they forced the not-so-docile Shetland up the ramp. He rode alone.

Upon reaching Virginia City, the "pet" was led into his new home, a shed. Immediately, he kicked down the feed trough. He kicked my father. And he kicked down the stable door. By this time, I had lost much of my enthusiasm.

However, by the next morning, our yard was filled with kids. They wanted to see me riding, and some thought that perhaps they would be offered a similar opportunity. With some opposition from the Shetland, a saddle was strapped on his back, and a halter placed on his head. The bit in his mouth did not deter him from trying to bite the nearby humans. With much urging, I got my foot in the stirrup, and was immediately bucked off.

I finally got mounted, and we trotted around the yard several times before I was bucked off again. Some of the older boys wanted to try a ride. They had a bit more success, especially Jack Flanagan, who enforced his commands with a two-foot section of garden hose.

I contacted Mr. Flanagan, retired Storey County assessor, the other day in Virginia City. He remembered the Shetland affair very vividly. "A mean, vicious little critter!" he recalled.

One teenager, Joe Fisher, had a successful ride temporarily. People thought the pony needed more exercise, and Joe rode him through the town and out the road toward Geiger Grade. He approached Livingstone Ravine, about two miles north, where they operated an old-fashioned hand laundry. Old Mrs. Livingstone had just hung out washed sheets, towels and other items on the wooden drying poles in the yard. The Shetland bolted off the road, galloped down the ravine, and carried his rider through the laundry, trailing sheets and towels through the sagebrush.

The last straw, so to speak, was in my last ride. I managed to steer the pony up past the Fourth Ward School, on to the Divide, where he bucked me off on a rocky street. He reared back and his hooves came down; I rolled out of range just in time. My dad advertised the pony for sale, and he was purchased by a rancher from Washoe Valley.

"I must warn you," said my dad, "that he's rather spirited and ornery."

"Oh, that's OK," replied the confident rancher. "I think we need some spirit in our herd." —*January 17, 1990*

I was on the squad, but that's a big difference from being a player

Just for the record—to be honest, I never played for the UNR Wolf Pack under coach Jake Lawlor. As a newsman, I covered hundreds of Wolf Pack basketball games during the Jake Lawlor era but did not play on those teams. Some readers say they got the impression that I did after reading biographical material.

Actually, however, I was on the squad of the first high school team Jake coached—at Virginia City, 1933.

That was all. I was on the squad, but that's a big difference from being a player. It was my senior year, and Jake carried an 11-man squad. And You Know Who was No. 11. There was the first team, the starters; and the second team, the five other substitutes; and No. 11. I guess Jake carried 11 men through kindness, because in basketball I had a big handicap—no ability. In addition to having bad hands—I dropped most of the passes thrown to me. To paraphrase an old cliché of sports—"I may have been small, but I was slow." Also nearsighted. Those were the days when players did not wear glasses in action, and having a center jump after each basket. There were signals as to where our center would try to tip the ball and the toss-up—such as waving three fingers in the air to indicate the right forward would try to get the ball being tipped. When you couldn't see clearly enough to be ready to grab the tips you messed up the play. Actually, we didn't get the center jump tip very often. In those days, anyone over six feet tall was regarded as a giant, and was destined to be a center, regardless of his jumping ability.

Jake Lawlor, legendary basketball coach of Wolf Pack teams—200 victories. I was on the first team he ever coached, at Virginia City High School.

My playing time in actual games varied with the score. If V.C. was way ahead (which wasn't often), the 11th man got in for a few minutes. Or if we were hopelessly behind, ditto. In the latter category, however, coach Jake Lawlor seldom resigned himself to defeat, figuring there was always some remote chance of a comeback.

When it came tournament time, the teams were limited to 10 players, and You Know Who didn't make the cut, or the trip.

Those were the days of "open" tournaments. And before the various divisions based on enrollments. Small schools like Virginia City competed with Reno, Las Vegas and the other biggies. And, in the years after I graduated, Virginia City, which usually had less than 20 boys in the entire student body, achieved remarkable performances. Jake Lawlor's subsequent teams went on to reach the state tournament semi-finals one year, and the state championship final in another! I repeat, this was AFTER my graduation; so that should be sufficient explanation.

Since development of the various divisions, Virginia City teams of Lyle Damon, Fred Gladding and other coaches won so many games and trophies that a lustre surrounds anyone who is an alumnus of the Comstock school. People sort of automatically believe that anyone in this category must have been a basketball star. I have often faced this situation, with a mild disclaimer, a modest "Well, yes, I was on the squad up there. When Jake coached, in fact." —*April 11, 1990*

A stroke of a miner's pick or drill could break open the earth and rock wall of the tunnel, and a jet of scalding liquid would shoot out

What is a Hot Water Plug? Many people are vaguely accustomed to that term but have no idea what it is, except that it is applied to Virginia City residents.

A Hot Water Plug was a miner who worked in the deepest levels of the vast mines of the 19th century, where the danger of encountering scalding hot water was always imminent.

Almost all the deep mines of the Comstock Lode were hot and moist. There were underground streams of boiling hot water coursing through the bowels of the old-time mines. A stroke of a miner's pick or drill could break open the earth and rock wall of the tunnel, and a jet of scalding liquid would shoot out. When this mishap occurred, the miners hastened to plug up the opening. Anything from slabs of rock to wooden barricades were shoved into the breech.

There was a report that bags of beans were also used, if the opening was not too large. The beans would swell up when placed against the watery opening, and would often work well as a temporary sealant.

The best hot water plugs were made of wood, shaped to fit perfectly into the holes in the "face" of the tunnel or drift. Bill Marks of the Crystal Bar used to exhibit one of these famous plugs left over from the old days.

Will Carroll, who compiled a great little book of Comstock anecdotes, reported how things were on the 2,700-foot level of the Con Virginia. He described a temporary ceiling device of canvas or sheet metal which shunted the stream of hot water away from the heads of the miners, keeping any squirts of hot water from hitting them.

My father recalled the heat in the Con Virginia was so stifling that one man was kept busy with a cold-water hose spraying a cooling mist over the bodies of the other miners.

My friend, retired Elko editor Chris Sheerin, described to his father a mishap in one of the deep mines. The engineer who operated the hoisting "cage" or elevator had to be extremely careful when lowering miners to the lowest levels. The hot water encountered in various levels was routed down to the bottom of the shaft. Here it formed a "sump" which was sometimes several feet deep in extremely hot water, often more than 120 degrees. (The water gathered here was later pumped to the surface via the great Cornish Pumps which carried vast amounts of water through a series of huge tanks at various levels.)

Sheerin recalled that his father and another miner were descending via the cage when the hoisting engineer accidentally lowered them into the sump! Sheerin, Sr. saved himself by pulling himself up to the bonnet (ceiling) of the cage but was severely burned up to his knees. The other miner did not manage to pull himself up, and he died.

To the southeast of Virginia City is a great mine dump which can be seen from the city. At one time, the Combination shaft was the deepest in the world. It was used jointly by four adjacent mines at the same time. It certainly encountered hot water, because I recall seeing from the Fourth Ward School in the 1930s huge clouds of steam billowing from the distant Combination shaft. After the famous shaft was abandoned, it was plugged up by various cave-ins.

The name Hot Water Plug has been carried on by the remaining natives of Virginia City, who are few in numbers now. The high school yearbook was called The Hot Water Plug for many years, but I understand the name was finally stopped in the early 1980s.

Well, that's what people mean by the name Hot Water Plug. Our numbers are dwindling, but we still use the name with fondness.

—*August 29, 1990*

Never even sneaked a peek, although I must confess to good peripheral vision at that time

There has been quite a flap in the news media lately about a woman sportwriter going into the men's dressing room to interview ball plaers.

This sort of incident occurs quite often, and there are heated discussions on the propriety of a female entering the place where players are dressing, undressing or coming out of the showers.

Somehow, I never heard of a male writer trying to get into the dressing room of female athletes.

I can empathize with the latter, however, because I was the only boy in high school to enter the girls' dressing room when it was full of unclad fems. It was strictly innocent, however, although it created a brief sensation (not physical).

In my junior year at Virginia City High School, the coaches appointed me and another boy to alternate on housewarming duties. The basketball games and practices were held in the old National Guard Hall, a large stone building used first as an armory back in the 1870s. It was heated by coal-burning stoves, a huge one in the big hall and a couple in the respective dressing rooms.

Our job was to walk downtown from the Fourth Ward School in mid-afternoon and start the fires in the stoves to warm up the dressing rooms and to warm the water for the showers. The girls held their practice sessions in late afternoon and we had the place cozy and warm for them.

However, one afternoon after the girls' practice, one opened their door and called: "Hey, Ty, we need more coal in here!" So I dutifully went to the coal bin, filled a bucket and knocked on the door of the dressing room.

Someone called, "Who is it?"

I answered, "It's Ty. I have brought the coal."

One senior player answered, "Well, bring it in!"

I figured she must know what they needed, so I opened the door and stepped in. Immediately there rose a clamor from a dozen unclad or half-clad females!

"Don't come in here!" shouted some of the shy ones.

"Bring it on in," advised the mischievous ones.

I kept going on in, directly to the stove, without looking to either side. Poured some coal into the stove and set down the bucket. Turned around and walked to the door, all the time looking straight ahead, like a gentleman. Never even sneaked a peek, although I must confess to good peripheral vision at that time.

Peals of laughter rang in my ears as I left the sanctum of athletic femininity.

Word of this affair quickly got around the school the next day, and I was besieged by boys asking, "What did you see?" "What about …— is she really …?"

Like a true gentleman, I parried the questions with negatives—"I cannot answer. I didn't see a thing."

And I will keep my secrets forever, like a true gentleman.

—October 31, 1990

His concern and compassion for others derived from his own hardships as a youngster

Every person thinks his Dad is Something Special. And we agree. We felt that way too. It would be great if every person had the medium of a newspaper column in which to recall his Dad's contributions. But, of course, that would be highly impractical. But since this writer does have that medium, it's a chance to say a bit more about a person who made many contributions to the well-being of his fellow citizens.

Will Cobb (who died Friday night) lived a full life during his 88 years in Nevada, and much of that time was devoted to improving the welfare of others. During a dozen years in the Nevada Legislature, he sponsored or supported social legislation which had a definite effect on the lives of thousands. Old age pensions, minimum wage, hunting-fishing privileges for the elderly, minimum wage for women, teachers' pensions, railroad train limit (crew safety), mine safety, pensions for the blind, and many others.

Perhaps his concern and compassion for others derived from his own hardships as a youngster. His father (who had been a teenage cavalryman in the Civil War, being wounded, captured and escaped from a Confederate prison) died when Will Cobb was only two. The widowed mother tried to support three small boys, but there were years in orphanages, curtailed education (he had to leave school in the sixth grade to work), and many privations. As a youngster, he was up at three o'clock in the morning to deliver the *Territorial Enterprise* in Virginia City; and as a teenager too young to work in the mines, he washed dishes in cafes of boomtowns Goldfield and Tonopah.

Like most Comstockers, he later worked in the deep mines, and recently recalled the heat in the C&C mine as so intense that "they sprayed us with a water hose while we worked in a drift." He was something of a daredevil, too. When some miners were dashed to their deaths in the shaft of the Union Mine, due to malfunction of the hoisting cage (elevator), Will Cobb and another young man volunteered to be lowered by cable to see if any aid could be given. The other young man was a University of California mining student named Doolittle, who was later to be known as General Jimmy Doolittle who led the first bombing raid on Tokyo, Japan, during World War II.

One of the old-timers' favorite stories was the baseball game on the Pan-Mill diamond when Will Cobb pitched for Dayton against his brother who hurled for Virginia City, and the rival brother-pitchers flared into a bean-ball sequence, knocking each other down with pitches throughout the game.

Will Cobb became a sort of legend as a bus driver, too, driving a square-built, jolting vehicle over the old (dirt) Geiger Grade as many as four to six round-trips a day. There weren't many state highway snow plows available in the 1920s and '30s, and often Cobb's bus kept the roads open during winter. On occasion, volunteers brought their shovels and rode along as he smashed through the snow drifts;

piling out to shovel it clear when the bus became stuck. He was influential in bringing about the modern Geiger Grade.

Later his route was extended from Reno to Lake Tahoe, bringing mail, freight and passengers to the South Shore. Those were the days of the Bliss family at Glenbrook, the Wileys at Zephyr, Youngs and Conollys at Bijou, Globin at Al Tahoe and the Richardsons at Camp Richardson. He frequently went far out of his way to deliver a package or traveler to remote Tahoe places. Now the South Shore has mushroomed into one continuous city, with individuality overwhelmed.

He never missed a day of travel, despite Tahoe winter conditions, sometimes battling Kings Canyon road when the old Clear Creek route was blockaded. Yet, in more than 30 years of driving, he never had a mishap, not even a fender-bender.

Will Cobb wielded rare power in the Legislature through its political makeup—almost an even division of Democrats and Republicans when, as an elected Independent, he held the tie-breaking vote. But he was unable to complete a state lottery plan to finance pensions. Nevertheless, he did establish awareness of the need for social legislation. Ironically, he himself never received benefits which latter-day legislators voted for themselves.

After further public service as sheriff-assessor and county commissioner, he lived out his remaining years in quiet dignity—continuing to be concerned about other elderly or ailing townspeople. Newcomers who came to participate in the modern tourist boom of the old mining camp were less aware of Will Cobb, but many others continued to regard him as Something Special. We did, too.

—*August 5, 1973*

He was noted as fearless in seizing the rattlers barehanded

If you read Robert Laxalt's second book "Man in a Wheat Field," you'll not soon forget the main character—the garage man who collected rattlesnakes.

For people with a western Nevada background, the site of the book was easily recognizable as Dayton, Nev., and even the characters bore names easily identified with people who lived in the little town on the Carson River.

While the garage man who gathered rattlers had a different name in the book, everyone knew he was the prototype of Chester (Monk) Barton. Mr. Barton, who died at age 80 last weekend, operated a small garage in Dayton, and not only collected rattlesnakes, but many other kinds of wildlife. He was noted as fearless in seizing the rattlers barehanded, and although he was bitten a few times, suffered no ill effects.

As one Dayton resident remarked last week, "Barton was everything to everyone in Dayton." He was a law enforcer, amateur doctor, interpreter (he spoke Paiute and Indian), mechanic, gardener adviser, etc.

We will remember him always for several minutes of terror in his backyard. As a small boy, about five or six, we were at Barton's while the parents visited. Wandering into the back of the garage, we became curious about a large box with a screen cover.

Lifting the lid, we were horrified to see a snarl of hissing, whirring *rattlesnakes* raising their heads at the intrusion. We slammed down the cover, with a screech of terror, and started to run. This stirred the curiosity of a big *coyote,* who pursued us as far as his tether would reach.

Trembling with fear, we dashed for the apparent safety of a big shed. We threw the door open, only to be confronted by a hiss and snarl from a *bobcat,* and a wing-flapping screech from a big *eagle!*

We fled the menagerie for the safety of the family truck. It was a long time afterward before we paid any more visits to Dayton, and then we steered clear of Barton's garage. —*September 9, 1973*

The chiropractor was fond of grappling without shoes, and his bare toes made good targets for a wily opponent

Mention of the Chestnut Street Arena stirs memories among local sports fans who attended boxing and wrestling shows in that compact pavilion during the early 1930s.

One of these days, we'll go into more detail about some of the rip-roaring fight cards held there. But the mention of the old Chestnut Street Arena wrestling cards, and the biggest drawing card, Peter Visser, also produced some ribald reminiscences.

The wrestling cards themselves were no different from those produced nowadays. There's the villain, a sneering monster who affects weird costumes and hair-dos, who inflicts all kinds of dirty tricks on the poor hero. And the same dumb referee, who just can't see how the villain is violating all the precepts of sportsmanship. And the hero, a handsome, clean-cut individual who undergoes unspeakable tortures and indignities at the hands of the bad guy until he just can't stand it any longer and, bursting in all his wrath from an illegal hold, he gives the evil fellow what-for.

Well, back in the early '30s, Dr. Peter Visser was the bad guy. Week after week, he'd come to Reno and torment the nice guys. The "doctor" in his name came, it was said, because he was reputed to be a chiropractor. Therefore, he had an unfair advantage, using this knowledge of human anatomy and its vulnerable and tender spots to bedevil the opponents. When he had an adversary on the mat, and the rival would writhe and howl, the fans would nudge each other and comment, "See, that's the secret chiropractor hold." Dr. Visser was fond of grappling without shoes, and his bare toes made good targets for a wily opponent.

The doctor was baldish, too. So, bare both top and bottom, he'd be prey for retaliation, and this made the Reno fans howl with delight. Visser was quite a one for leaving the ring and roaming through the arena, even way up in the cheap seats, either in pursuit of or in flight from, an opponent. Quite often he'd grab a water bucket with which to pursue the foe up and down the aisles.

The water bucket chase reminds us of another Chestnut Street legend—the Great Chair Switch. We do not know if Dr. Visser was involved in this incident. But it has been repeated and passed down many times over the ensuing 45 or so years.

As the apparent mayhem grew more flamboyant each week, someone in the promotion line figured out a real doozie. The idea was to have one wrestler bash another over the head with a chair. Now, to make sure that the chair would splinter in spectacular fashion, without actually caving in the cranium of the "victim," a chair was doctored up earlier in the day. Someone, so the story goes, carefully sawed well into all of the legs of the chair. Not right through, but almost, leaving enough intact to keep it from falling apart right then. As it was one of those lightweight chairs with slim slats instead of solid seat and back, the slats, too, were sawed almost through.

The plan was to leave the flimsy chair next to ringside where, as ring action reached a crescendo of excitement, one wrestler was to go through the ropes and grasp the chair. He was then to smash it over the head of the opponent, and it was supposed to shatter into a dozen pieces, to the awe of the customers.

This was a great plan.

However, the night of the wrestling match, some fan tried to sit in the sawed-through chair. It was rescued by an usher, just in time, and he moved it to a place more out of reach. Unfortunately, there was another chair at ringside, unoccupied, which looked just like the doctored-up seat. In the heat of battle, the wrestler went down and grabbed this one—the unsawed, sturdy chair. And he swung it onto the head of his opponent.

Instead of the expected shattering of the chair into many pieces, there was only the sodden thunk of a solid piece of furniture conking the unfortunate victim. The swinger stood gaping in amazement, an intact chair still in his hands. Surprised and dazed, blood streaming from the top of his head, the recipient staggered around.

We understand he was treated at St. Mary's Hospital, luckily only a couple of blocks away. And the episode of the Switched Chair lives on as a tribute to realism in wrestling. —*April 23, 1978*

Bill Cobb, my son, left; President Ronald Reagan, and Cobb.

The clatter of sticks banging on garbage can lid shields aroused the neighbors, who aroused the law

We have noticed with surprise signs of construction activity in a Southeast Reno locale. No surprise at the bulldozers and cement mixers, because they're hardly a surprise in any part of Reno now. But the location has been vacant so long it just didn't seem like it would ever be used.

That's the big lot between Wells and Wheeler avenues, and Crampton and Burns streets, a very large area which remained vacant even when Burke's Addition was developed back in the earlier days of Reno. It was an empty area surrounded by residences back in the 1920s, when this writer, as a youngster, moved to Reno for a five-year period.

As a vacant lot, this was the king of 'em all.

It was a super place for kite flying. You could let out all the string on your roll and still stay within bounds. Or, if a kite did get away after a string broke, you had a good chance of retrieving it because there weren't many houses on the east side of Wells Avenue.

What made the lot most attractive to the small boys of the neighborhood, however, was the "bushes." There was a long streak of some peculiar bush growing in the lot, stretching from the southeast corner near the Herz home all the way to Wheeler Avenue. The growth was as tall as a man and several feet wide, enough to permit enterprising boys to fashion "jungle" paths, dugouts, hideouts. A great place for a juvenile Tom Mix or Hoot Gibson, or Tarzan—depending whether you attended the Majestic or Wigwam theater last—to hide from the bad guys.

This part of the Lot was also the site of brief gang warfare. The Burke's Addition Gang engaged in battle with the Mill Street Gang, which made the cross-town foray on bikes and a stripped-down Ford Model T "bug" for a brief encounter. The clatter of sticks banging on garbage can lid shields aroused the neighbors, who aroused the Law. The gladiators were dispersed, and then the fire department came to burn away all those beloved bushes, which never returned.

As the years, and generations, rolled by the huge lot remained vacant, surprising in a growing city. We always understood it belonged to Lavere Redfield, who on occasion was persuaded to allow temporary recreation ventures on the site. These were short-lived. The field had always had some baseball activity such as "One Ol' Cat," but when construction of a junior baseball park was proposed, neighbor objections prevailed.

Then there was the time when someone thought it would be a good place for outdoor skating for the kids. Someone dozed up dirt sides for a skating pond, which the firemen then filled with water. The water, unfortunately, never froze hard enough to serve as a skating rink.

Well, the super vacant lot is giving way to modern construction. Office buildings will eventually grace the long-empty site of kites, Tarzans, Tom Mix, gladiators and the other long-vanished vestiges of childhood. —*April 30, 1978*

It wasn't easy to put the outfit together

The trouble with a Sunday column, many mid-week happenings are previously covered in the press. That's the case with the MGM-Grand opening in Reno Wednesday; the news media already thoroughly covered the glittering opening spectacle.

However, there is one facet which we intend to dwell upon. The impact of the MGM giant on Reno traffic, labor market, ecology, sociology, etc., has also been studied in-depth.

But the impact we intend to discourse on is tuxedo attire.

When Jack Pieper sent out his invitations to several hundred Western Nevada people for the all-local opening affair on Wednesday, the cards added simply "Black Tie Optional."

We wondered briefly what was the fuss about a black necktie, then we realized the man was telling guests to doll up, come formal. This was no problem to some Renoites who already owned tuxedoes. Some lodge men have had 'em for years. And the recent emphasis on culture in Reno—the symphony-opera cult—has prodded others to acquire formal attire. However, the large majority of Reno men are lacking the fancy layouts in their closets. Fortunately, several clothing shops provide rent-a-tux service and these did a rip-roaring business in the last two weeks.

Personally, we approached the tuxedo problem with misgivings. The horrors of men's formal suits back in our college days are still deeply etched, even after four decades.

You just didn't rent a tux back in those days, and borrowing one was an ordeal almost as harrowing as the donning and wearing. When a young lady invited us to a sorority "formal" dance, this green freshman from the hills was terrified. But friends set out to gather an outfit—borrowing a pair of pants from the Sigma Phi house, getting an appropriate fit of a jacket from the ATO's, learning of a spare "hard-boiled" shirt at the SAE house and a stiff collar someone had over at the Phi Sigs. A Lambda Chi was persuaded to loan his cufflinks and studs, and the whole operation was completed by an entourage of advisers at the Sigma Nu digs.

It wasn't easy putting the outfit together. In those days, the stiff collar and the boiled shirt were separate and had to be fastened together. And the black bow tie, unlike the hundreds sported at MGM the other night, weren't of the easy clip-on type. You had to tie a real bow. Bill Beemer was the only man in our house who could properly tie a bow tie which wouldn't come unraveled the minute the dance began, so we had to wait for him to arrive to apply the permanent knot. Many a luckless youth lost his dapper look within minutes of arriving at the sorority dance, his bow tie coming unstrung and hanging down, his collar separating from the shirt, with other misfortunes. (It could have been worse. In previous years, a "hard-boiled shirt" came with a stiffly-starched front, or dicky, which flew up like a window shade.)

Thank goodness, the sorority "formal" finally came to an end, and the disheveled youths took their long-gowned dates home. Personally, we avoided any more "formals" for the next three years.

—*May 7, 1978*

Harrah's passion was fast cars

We last saw Bill Harrah the night MGM opened in Reno. He was standing just outside the Grand Ballroom, looking over the crowd which, including himself, had come for the First Night of his new business rival. He introduced us to his party with, "I want you to meet Ty Cobb, one of my first, oldest and best friends in Reno."

Well stated. Our acquaintance with Bill Harrah dated back to 1937, the year we started working for the *Nevada State Journal*. The same year Bill, his father John Harrah, and best friend Bob Ring came to Reno to start a modest little bingo parlor on Center Street. Gambling then was concentrated within two or three blocks of downtown Reno. The Bank Club on Center Street at Douglas Alley dominated Reno. Who would have thought then that the site of the once-mighty Bank Club, plus the locales of the Golden Hotel, Northern Club, Grand Cafe and Hotel, Reno Florist, drug store and other shops would some day all be occupied by a giant Harrah casino-hotel?

The first little bingo parlor was so modest that they didn't even have a safe; after closing each night, they left their receipts and "bank-roll" in the safe of the nearby Wine House.

We got to know Bill Harrah best when he made his hangout the 116 Club, now the Stein Hof-Brau at 116 N. Center St. Just after midnight, the newsmen had just put the morning *Journal* to bed and while waiting for it to roll off the press next door, they'd cool off with a beer or two in the 116. It was also the quiet relaxing spot for waiters, dealers, bartenders and others who had just completed the night shift.

Among this group of nighthawks was Bill Harrah, usually accompanied by his partner Bob Ring. Harrah always took a stool at the far end of the bar and, although he seldom said anything, seemed to like hearing the others. He liked the company of two waiters from the Town House, a popular club on West First Street (where J.C. Penney now stands).

Harrah's passion was fast cars. He loved speed, which proved his undoing in at least one major auto wreck. For months he walked around, head stiffly high, due to a brace which supported a badly damaged neck. This bearing gave him a somewhat "distant" appearance, which was mistaken by some as aloofness.

Later he transferred his interest in autos from driving fast ones to collecting old ones. He started acquiring and restoring ancient automobiles, with an obsession for authenticity. Liked to drive the old cars, too, and he was a prime force in organizing and leading the horseless carriage club and its activities. Some of his friends and associates took up the fad, and elderly Duesenbergs, Stanley Steamers and Whites were no novelty chugging around Reno streets. Bill Harrah was in his happiest moments when the horseless carriage club ran expeditions to Virginia City or Lake Tahoe, the drivers and passengers all togged out in authentic clothing of the early 1900s. We enjoyed those junkets as a guest of Harrah, looking dashing in the togs of the "Good Old Days." This hobby led to Harrah creating his fabulous auto museum, the greatest of its kind in the world.

His yen for speed had long worn off when he assumed a new role, that of sponsor, in boat racing. He took up sponsorship of unlimited hydroplane racing, helping to support some of the Gold Cup thrillers at Lake Tahoe and sending his own entry after glory in the expensive and dangerous sport. His organization backed a speedy hydro re-named "Harrah's Tahoe Miss" which campaigned on the circuit with mixed success. Suddenly, Harrah lost interest in the sport and dropped the whole project.

We saw less of him as the years went on, as Bill concentrated on expanding his empire, but still shying away from the public eye. However, we can't forget a street conversation in 1960, just after our promotion to managing editor of the *Journal*. "So they finally made you an editor," he commented. "Congratulations." Then he added an afterthought as he continued down the street. "About time."

Now he's being eulogized, and quite properly, by the giants of government, entertainment and business. We'll always remember him as the *Quiet Man* we knew 40 years ago.—*July 2, 1978*

Subscriptions were paid for with six chickens, a cord of wood, or much credit

A milestone in Nevada journalism was quietly reached recently.

Walter and Vivian Cox sold their remaining interest in the *Mason Valley News* of Yerington to Jim Sanford, son of Bob and Martha Sanford, who have been co-publishers of the lively weekly since 1958.

This action concluded the interests of the Cox family which had been associated with the *Mason Valley News* for 60 years.

Frank Cox, Walter's father, had been a publisher in Virginia City, then was with the *San Francisco Examiner.* He came to Mason Valley in 1907, installed the first linotype machine in the *Yerington Times* plant. As a boy of 10, Walter Cox began in "journalism" by folding papers, later graduated to janitor and printer's devil (helper).

About this time, the Great Depression hit Nevada full force and the bank closure found the newspaper firm with just $5 in cash. In those days, however, W. Cox recalls, many subscriptions were paid for with "six chickens, a cord of wood, or much credit."

Thinking he would be helpful, the young Walter spent a weekend painting the walls of the newspaper office. But the senior Cox was not pleased when he entered the place Monday morning. He slammed his hat to the floor and roared, "You have destroyed three years of book-keeping."

Eventually Walter became head of the paper and also took an active role in affairs of Lyon County, ranging from the water board to serving in the state Senate. In 1945, he took a partner, Jack Carpenter of Fallon, who was co-publisher until he went to Washington, D.C., as an aide for Senator Alan Bible. In those days, Walter recalls, "you got the latest news by calling Central (telephone operator) and asking her."

Bob Sanford, formerly of Fallon, later of Tonopah, and his wife, Martha, moved to Yerington in 1958 and acquired a half interest in the paper. The energetic Sanfords built their local coverage to amazing proportions, ignoring the time-honored rules of publishing—more advertising than news space. Elder son Jim Sanford helped build the paper. When this writer was managing editor of the *Journal*, one of the best UNR interns we had was Jim Sanford. He resisted our job offer and went back to help his folks. The Sanfords have been rewarded with numerous state press awards and honors. Meanwhile they built their coverage of Fernley, Silver Springs, Dayton, Smith Valley, and lately, Silver City and Virginia City. Even started publishing a new Fallon newspaper. And younger son Dave is in the sports editing end.

Walter Cox has enjoyed semi-retirement by writing his homespun weekly column, Cox's Column, which is adorned with a sketch of a rooster, and by gallivanting around the world. He most recently took a tour through China and presumably advised the Celestials on irrigation and hot-type printing.

Meanwhile, the publication continues to flourish its printed slogan: "The Only Newspaper in the World That Gives a Damn About Yerington." —*January 30, 1980*

*The G-man was tracking down
the rumor that mobster Baby Face Nelson
was hiding out in western Nevada*

A friend watching an old "FBI" televi-
sion episode the other night was re-
minded of something from Reno's past.
He recalled the heyday of the first FBI
agent locally.

John McLaughlin died five years ago
after serving as U.S. magistrate for this
area. His family survives him and lives
on in Reno. The McLaughlins were
best known locally for their beautiful
residence high on California Avenue.

But the late John McLaughlin was
something of a legend himself. He was
one of the first "G-Men" when J. Edgar
Hoover reorganized the Federal Bureau
of Investigation and took after a crop
of notorious interstate mobsters.
McLaughlin was in on the pursuit of
the infamous Alvin Karpis, Ma Barker,
John Dillinger, Machine Gun Kelly and
other gangsters.

In fact, it was said that McLaughlin was in the FBI net that closed
on John Dillinger (fatally) in Chicago. McLaughlin was reputed to be
the agent assigned to protect the "Lady in Red" when the female tip-
ster emerged from the Chicago movie theater in company with
Dillinger.

McLaughlin was the first FBI agent sent to the Reno area by Hoover,
and he recalled that his initial visit was not popular with some locals.
He said, years later, that when he arrived, he was met by a delegation
of Reno citizens, including some law enforcement people, who told
him flatly he was not welcome—and advised him to keep moving.

The G-Man complied, taking the same train on out of town. But he promptly returned, inconspicuously, on the next train back, and went about his assigned business. That was to track down the rumor that mobster Baby Face Nelson and friends were hiding out in western Nevada. That was reputed to be at Walley's Hot Springs near Genoa.

His mission completed, agent McLaughlin remained on in Reno, and his work was made easier by a wave of help "from the reform element" here, he later said.

One of the agent's favorite anecdotes concerned the late multi-millionaire Max Fleischmann. The retired manufacturer lived at Lake Tahoe (Round Hill) where his hobby was playing cop. He had been given an honorary deputy sheriff's badge from Douglas County and prized it to the extent of stopping speeders on the south shore highway.

One time, FBI agent McLaughlin was tailing a suspect at Tahoe who was traveling rapidly, forcing the pursuer to exceed the speed limit, too. To his dismay, the G-Man was overhauled and forced to halt by a flashing red light and a wailing siren. The pursuer proved to be the elderly millionaire Fleischmann. Hastily, McLaughlin identified himself and explained his chase of the car ahead. Honorary deputy Fleischmann exclaimed: "Come on—let's go get him!"

We have never learned if the suspect got away or was eventually chased down by the distinguished lawmen. —*February 24, 1980*

He was a model of deportment for all us other diners

Remember the old song about: "There'za Small Hotel…?"

It came to mind when Walter Cox, in the *Mason Valley News,* revealed that the historical Brooks Home Cottage had changed hands.

He noted, "Mary E. Smith will receive the keys from Mr. and Mrs. Joe Menesini. Correction: the hotel never had a key to the front door."

The building was erected by Mary E. Brooks in 1907 and she operated it for more than half a century. Cox recalled there was a barn and a feed corral in back. "It was the custom for traveling salesmen to hire a team and buckboard at Wabuska after alighting from the train, and drive the 12 miles to Yerington …"

Mary Brooks was a very strict innkeeper, Walter reminisces, "and out you went if liquor was found in your room, or a fair damsel was caught visiting with the door closed. It was years before pollution— but to light a cigar, pipe or cigarette in that dining room was a cardinal sin, and you were no longer welcome …. The hotel was generally filled with farmers and their families in town for the holiday dances, traveling salesmen, teachers, an occasional doctor …."

To which he can add, also with highwaymen.

Not bandits, but highwaymen who worked for the state highway department and construction crews. This writer spent a summer at Mrs. Brooks' little hotel and still has fond memories of the place and the kindly little lady who operated it.

In the summer of 1935, we had employment on the highway. They were building the paved highway from near Wabuska, across the desert for many miles north toward Fernley. (Silver Springs hadn't been thought of then.)

That job was handled by the Tedford Construction Co. of Fallon, which worked from dawn until dark. Our particular job was weigh-master. We weighed the loads of sand, gravel, etc., which came out of the Tedford camp rock crushers and were applied to the road surface. First, we'd weigh the empty trucks which drove across our portable scales. Later, we weighed the loaded trucks and subtracted, to get the load weight.

It was such a long work day we split the weighing chores with Tuffy Congdon of Carson, who was also our roommate at Mrs. Brooks', he had the early shift and we took the late one, which meant we didn't get back to the hotel in Yerington, 15 or 20 miles away, until around 8 o'clock at night. Nevertheless, kindly Mrs. Brooks always kept a hot dinner in her kitchen, warming in the huge coal range where she fixed hearty fare for her boarders.

Her dining room was spotless, the linen snowy white and as Cox mentioned, you minded your manners. This was a pleasure to Mr. Amby Kramer, who worked as flagman on the road construction. He had elegant manners such as keeping his napkin on his lap instead of his neck or shirt front. He was a model of deportment for all us other diners. Mr. Kramer's existence was blighted by the crazy speeding tourists who often nearly ran him down as he tried to signal them to slow down on the construction project.

The construction job was a hot and very dusty one, and we all gave Mrs. Brooks' bathtubs heavy use. Man, was it hot out there on the desert! And the weird winds blew dust and sand everywhere. We'll always remember the fate of one morning's work when the camp was hit by a "dust devil."

We were plagued by violent whirlwinds. One windy morning, the Tedford people had worked hours at their rock crusher, grinding gravel into soft sand. This was carried by a conveyor belt up to an overhead bin, from there to be loaded into the trucks. On this very windy morning, we all observed a large and vigorous whirlwind coming through the sagebrush. Its swirling currents sucked up desert sand, weeds and brush until it looked like a miniature tornado.

The workmen watched with apprehension as it neared the Tedford camp. "Oh, no!" groaned the foreman as the whirlwind went straight for the overhead bin of sand. As if guided by some devilish force, it not only went right for the sand bin, it stopped there. Stayed there until every grain of sand—so painfully produced by those hours at the rock crusher, was sucked up into the cloud of dust whirling away up there. Then it continued on out into Lyon County, somewhere, spewing its ill-gotten load over the landscape. And leaving the sorrowful workers to start all over again.

Yerington in '35 didn't have much recreation for a teenage "outsider." Luckily, we had some friends in the community—Carol Fabri, whose folks had a furniture store, university football player Joe Lommori, Bill Rawson who later was chief of police, and others. There was a pool hall, and a tri-weekly movie. After all, a youth working a late shift six days a week, finishing dinner at Mrs. Brooks, home about 9 p.m., and observing the decorum (Mrs. Brooks was a mother in a home away from home) had a chance to save up money for the next semester's expenses.

And after all, we were being paid a princely five dollars a day!

—July 20, 1980

His open palm smacked
sharply against the back of the boy's head

A persistent problem of modern education is the question of punishment of unruly students in schools. School boards, superintendents and principals continually face this dilemma: should a nasty youngster be spanked? Yes, agree many of the teachers plagued with smart-aleck pupils. "Spare the rod and spoil the child," they say, repeating the old adage.

"Don't you dare land a hand on my little darling!" respond the indignant parents. They, and some of the "liberal" educators, insist that physical punishment is not only cruel, but could affect the students' personalities, etc., in future years.

We're not going to preach on either theory. We're just going to recall an incident of more than four decades ago.

It was back around 1932 when a new teacher arrived at the high school in Virginia City. A new part of the three-teacher faculty in the old Fourth Ward School was young John Gilmartin, fresh out of college. He was to be an instructor as well as athletic coach. Tall and wiry, he had been a fine athlete at University of Nevada (Reno, of course), playing center on the Wolf Pack basketball team and holder of the university high jump record in track. He was also exceptionally quiet, perhaps nervous over his first teaching job. (He was later to coach at Wadsworth, which no longer has a high school, and was principal at Gerlach before his death several years ago.)

Probably the boys of Virginia City High School mistook Gilmartin's quiet manner for timidity. Anyway, they decided to test him and tease him. They wised-off and were sassy. They made silly and rude remarks.

The new teacher flushed with irritation, but remained calm. He politely asked them to "knock it off." This warning was not effective. The lads missed the soft steel in the teacher's voice.

Then he spoke up, more loudly, "This is the last warning!"

In that classroom, which had been constructed to accommodate six or seven times more pupils, the boys were concentrated in two rows of desks.

WHACK! His open palm smacked sharply against the back of the first boy's head. SMACK! his other hand popped the head of the neighboring youth. Up the aisle the teacher strode, whopping the back of every head with a stinging smack. A smart-ass kid's face went down on his desk so sharply that his nose bled.

Teacher Gilmartin, his chastisement completed, stood in front of his amazed adversaries and stated, "Now—go home and tell your parents that I hit you. Then they can call the school board and get me fired."

Not one did. Not a single one of the smacked smarties ever told his parents. There was never a discipline problem the rest of the year. And the following year Gilmartin was appointed principal.

As far as we can recall, none of those boys was ever suspended or expelled. And in later life, none of them ever made a jail or courtroom. —*September 24, 1980*

There was a tremendous blast, almost of nuclear power

Jim Herz really spilled the beans. He dusted off a half-century-old incident concerning *our* cooking ability.

Speaking at the recent Boy Scout Recognition dinner during which he took part in awarding of the belated (52 years) Eagle Badge to yours truly, he digressed from the ceremony to remind us, and everyone present, of the great Bean Explosion.

It occurred during one of our lengthy hikes in the fledgling Scout days, when we were working for Tenderfoot or Second Class badges. We toted along a can of pork 'n beans as subsistence during the lengthy walk into the foothills. We didn't quite cook 'em right. Jim Herz says we neglected to open, or punch a hole in the can of beans. Our recollection was that we stuck the cover on the cooking pot too tightly. (Or maybe that was another time.) Anyway, the pent-up steam inside the can/pot exploded. There was a tremendous blast, almost of nuclear power. The hungry Scouts around the campfire were showered with hot beans, bits of pork, bits of pot or can, plus embers from the campfire.

That incident ranks with another which we recall was also of atomic bomb stature. On another hike, we stopped for a meal and started a campfire. True to Scout safety teaching, we lined the fireplace with rock. There were numerous flat slabs of shale nearby, and we walled the fire with these handy pieces. A roaring fire was started, working down to red-hot embers and coals. We hung the cooking pots over the glowing fire and sat back in anticipation of a hot meal. Suddenly there was a loud pop, accompanied by a spray of shrapnel-like pieces of the shale slabs. Followed by another, and another. And another, with the fireplace "wall" scattered, along with some of our meal, into flying pieces of rock. Apparently shale has internal pockets of air or gas which remain there for centuries, until some unsuspecting kids put it against a roaring fire. Then the internal pocket of vapor gets so over-heated it explodes!

We eventually learned to puncture food cans, to loosen pot lids, and not to use shale for fireplaces. We went on to such heights as qualifying for the Cooking merit badge. But we did experience some discomfort with "twist," which does not refer to the dance of the same name.

"Twist," as many outdoorsmen know, is a method of cooking "bread" when you are out in the wilderness and far from a bakery. It consists of a gob of bread dough, rolled out in the form of a two-foot rope. This is then twisted around a stick, elevated over a bed of fiery coals, and baked. Convenient, and fairly tasty, if you're hungry enough from hiking. Our first problem with "Twist" was that the stick on which the rope dough was coiled was so dry that it caught fire, burned the dough and fell into the fire.

Later we decided to use greener sticks and cut a suitable branch from a tree. With the soft bark still on it. The trouble here was that the branch did not burn, but the sap and juices within it oozed out, impregnated the dough and gave the delicacy a God-awful taste.

We also recall another outdoorsy incident from our earlier Scout days. Our patrol, from Troop One, set out on an overnight hike toward Hunter Creek. We tramped through the city, and out Mayberry Road, until we reached the Mayberry Ranch. Only a few minutes auto drive now, over the four-lane highway, but it seemed like a great distance then for small boys to tramp. We turned up the canyon above the ranch, and hiked until we reached a shelter. This bore the colorful name of "Black Hawk Lodge," but was really just a lean-to of old and dry pine branches. After an uncomfortable night, the next morning we decided to hike further up the mountain toward Hunter Lake. Neglecting to bring along any food, we scrambled up the hill until we reached the reservoir, which was embellished by a wood-log dam. Pangs of hunger were gripping us hikers, but patrol leader Wayne Poulsen scoffed. "We'll just catch some trout and cook 'em," he stated confidently. We pointed out we had no fishing tackle, but he snorted that a good Scout could catch fish with a safety pin and string. For hours, we dangled this apparatus under the noses of some tiny fish which lurked in the weeds near the log dam. They disdained it, and we hungrily tramped back down to camp, wondering how the Indians and pioneer woodsmen would have done it. —*March 20, 1983*

Divested of her bloomers, the embarrassed young woman had little choice

During the 1983 Nevada state basketball tournament, Brickie Hanson found a pass to tourney games. He came across a large round button, which had belonged to his sister Ethel, on which was inscribed: "Delegate, Nevada State Tournament."

However, Mr. Hanson did not use the admission button to attend the '83 high school games. For one thing, the games were played in Las Vegas. For another, his admission button was for the 1924 tournament!

However, the 59-year-old souvenir did bring back memories for Brickie Hanson, who played basketball in Lovelock from 1925 to 1929. He got to thinking about girls basketball, too. Noting the skill and power of such present-day teams as the Reno and Carson City high school lady quintets, he agreed that feminine basketball has come a long way.

In the 1920s, the female version was a dull, confined game. Instead of the full-court style now used, the gals used a court divided (by painted lines on the floor) into three zones. There were six players to a side, two forwards, two guards and two centers (a jumper and a side center). Each pair was confined to its respective zones. The guards guarded, the forwards did all the shooting, and the centers simply jumped and relayed the ball.

One event the modern game has not equaled yet, however, was the startling streak of the streaker of some 60 (or so) years ago. As Brickie Hanson recalls the incident, which he witnessed in amazement, someone "pulled a bloomer."

This bloomer event does not refer to a miscue or error. It refers to a garment. In the 1920s, the young ladies playing basketball did not wear athletic shorts such as those worn by the present-day hoopsters. They wore a voluminous garment called "bloomers." It started at the waist and descended to the knee region, with quite a bit of cloth flowing out between. Presumably, the huge and loose panties were held up by rubberized waistbands.

"As I recall it," states ex-Lovelocker Hanson, "this girl was involved in a scramble for the basketball. And her bloomers fell down!" Furthermore, relates the eye witness of the embarrassing incident, the other girl in the scramble accidentally stepped on the fallen bloomers, pulling them completely off the victim!

Do you remember the quaint fad of a few years back when daring gals or guys peeled off their clothes and dashed, bare, in front of crowds of spectators at various events? They were called "streakers."

The embarrassed young woman who was divested of her bloomers in that long-ago basketball game had little choice. She could have re-donned the lost garment in front of all those spectators. But that would have been a devastating experience. Instead, she streaked the length of the basketball court and headed for the dressing room. We did not learn when, or if, she ever returned to the game. —*April 17, 1983*

Nevada native had guts to
tell off 'Blood and Guts' Patton

General George Patton was a tough guy. He was the hard-boiled, aggressive commander of mobile American armies, leading fast-moving forces on daring forays in Sicily, France and Germany. "Old Blood and Guts" Patton was fearless and hard-nosed.

No one, except a few of his military peers of superior rank, dared question his actions—much less someone of lesser military rank daring to "tell him off." Except for one man—a doctor from Reno, who had the nerve to scold the tough general.

The famous incident in World War II when Patton slapped a soldier in a hospital is well known, both to people who heard and read the news at that time, and the millions more who recently saw George C. Scott portray Patton in the movie of that name. Fewer people know that Dr. Frank Y. Leaver, a Nevada native, was the doctor who dared to bawl out the commanding general.

Leaver died a short time ago at Cape Cod, Mass., at the age of 80. Born in Virginia City, he was educated in Reno schools and the University of Nevada, also getting degrees at Harvard and Northwestern.

After the war, Leaver was associated with hospitals in Boston, San Francisco, Denver and Germany, usually in charge of training of radiologists. However, during World War II, he commanded combat hospitals in Africa, Sicily and at Anzio Beach in Italy. He was in charge of the 95th Evacuation Hospital near Gila, Sicily, where the famous Patton incident occurred.

Patton visited the Army hospital where he spoke with several patients. One of them was a Private Paul Bennett, who was hospitalized for battlefield emotional and mental fatigue. In his tough-talking style, the fiery general asked the soldier if he was eager to get back to combat. No sir, the private responded, he did not want to return to the battlefield.

Whereupon the commanding general hauled off and struck the patient twice on his face. The incident made headlines everywhere. Most readers were shocked. Patton himself was reprimanded by his superiors. What most people did not know was that the doctor from Reno confronted the crusty general in that hospital in Sicily immediately after the slapping incident and scolded him. Leaver reportedly told the general: "Do not return to my hospital unless you can act like a gentleman."

History does not tell us how Patton acted to this audacious remark by a subordinate. And Leaver himself wondered about the future of his own career. After all, you just don't tell off your Army commander, especially such a fiery person as "Blood and Guts" Patton. Apparently, Patton did not retaliate.

And later, the overall Allied commander, General Dwight Eisenhower, called Leaver to Rome and awarded him the Legion of Merit medal. —*May 1, 1983*

At least eight youths could perch on the running boards

At times when we pass local high school buildings, we are always amazed at the number of autos in the parking lots. It seems as if almost every student has a car. Which is all right, since there are considerable distances now from their homes to the schools, and it seems to us that classes start earlier in the mornings than we recall.

At the same time, we think back to our own high school days and the "Market Street Bus."

This venerable vehicle was a familiar sight in Virginia City, especially during the 1930s. It was remarkable for its carrying capacity. "The Market Street Bus" belonged to Robert Davis of Gold Hill, who worked as a mechanic in George Harris' garage.

In those days, high school students at the old Fourth Ward School seldom brought their lunches to school. Most of them went home for the noon meal, walking the mile or more to their residences, gulping the chow and trudging back to class. Sometimes this rapid walk was relieved by a free ride downtown on the Market Street Bus. Sometimes Bobby Davis would be passing the school on his way back to work and would stop to give the boys a lift.

And what a load it was!

How the roomy vehicle got its nickname is not certain. It was not a bus, but it certainly could carry a bus-sized load of passengers. It was a Dodge touring car of at least 1928 vintage. It was large. The back seat held four men comfortably, who could hold four more on their laps. Two or three more could pile in front with the driver. And in the back "cabin" there were foldout "jump seats" which could accommodate three or four more passengers. The "bus" had large and sturdy "running boards." These were iron steps outside the chassis, intended as stepping aids for people entering or leaving the car. But they were also good to stand on, if you were a high school student hooking a ride downtown on an already-overloaded auto. Often at least eight or 10 more youths could perch on the running boards, bringing the total load to 15 or 16 riders! (Modern law enforcement or traffic police would be horrified at this sight and would have quickly halted the expedition.)

But Virginia City police were tolerant in those Depression days. After all, as far as we can remember, only one student owned his own car, which he needed to deliver newspapers.

Some people did gape in amazement as the Market Street Bus crammed with half the male student body from the Fourth Ward. We think the "bus" also was equipped with a horn that sounded like a melodious whistle which identified it from afar. This, plus the shouts and chants from the massed riders, certainly let the downtowners know the Market Street Bus was coming!

For regular travel, however, the big touring car made many trips between Virginia City and Reno, Carson, Fallon and other sites. Sometimes it was carrying a group to a movie, or an athletic team or group of rooters to a faraway ball game. It could tote an entire basketball team, and the Virginia town team (Eagles) usually played rival "townies" at the same sites where the high school cagers were scheduled. It also bore entire baseball teams and equipment as far as Lovelock and Yerington. Owner-driver Bobby Davis had one requirement. He was adamant about the number "13" and would not allow a cargo of 13 riders. Twelve was OK, and also 14. Not 13.

Since Mr. Davis was an expert mechanic (he later worked many years in that capacity in Reno and is now retired), the Market Street Bus was kept in top mechanical condition. However, the tires of the early 1930s were not as durable as those nowadays.

On one occasion, either at Lovelock or Fernley, a much-patched tire blew out. It was beyond redemption and so was the spare, if there was a spare. Looking about, the lads saw a parked car of identical vintage as the Comstock touring car. They approached, jacked it up and switched their worn-out tire with the new rubber on the local auto— then merrily drove away.

There are many incidents connected with the noted Market Street Bus and we wish we could tell all. Including the time when, roaring down the desert highway toward Fallon, the car's radiator boiled over and all its water geysered away in a stream. How it was replenished cannot be told in a newspaper for the home. —*July 31, 1983*

It was with high hopes that the Country Club's silent backers watched the gala opening on June 26, 1935

It was all gone in two hours. Roaring flames had lighted the late-night sky over the south Reno area and quickly consumed what had been Reno's newest and most luxurious night club. After less than a year of existence, the Reno Country Club was destroyed.

Now, people driving along south Plumas Street not far from Moana Lane and adjoining Washoe County Golf Course may glance at the remnants of a stone wall, pieces of concrete foundation, and the stub of what had been a handsome fireplace chimney.

Those ruins are all that remain of the Country Club, plus some memories of older, longtime residents who recall the plush enterprise of the mid-1930s.

The Reno Country Club was opened on June 26, 1935. It perished on May 15, 1936.

A few golfers are still around who recall playing on the old Reno golf course and using its clubhouse which stood near Plumas Street (far from the present clubhouse of the Washoe County Golf Course, on a hilltop about a mile west).

During the late 1920s and early '30s, the Reno Golf Club's building was used by golfers and for social events until it was damaged by fire. Repaired, it again served until the Great Depression put a damper on organized golf. It was closed in 1932.

The site was leased by a group of Reno men "who preferred not to have their names published," according to a newspaper report, with intent to construct a super night club. Most of the financing, however, came from Lewis Luckenbach of the San Francisco-New York steamship line.

Cost of the enterprise was estimated at about $225,000, including construction and furnishings. At today's currency value, that would be up in the "several millions" bracket.

In spite of the Depression, Reno had an attraction for wealthy divorcees and was a mecca for high-rollers, since gambling had been legalized in Nevada a few years before. And Las Vegas as a gambling capital was hardly on the map.

So it was with high hopes that the Country Club's silent backers watched the gala opening on June 26, 1935.

Everyone attending agreed it was the most elaborate, luxurious place of its kind in the West. Guests approaching via the concrete driveway were greeted by a doorman and the new manager, Charlie Rennie. (His association with the country club was brief, however, and he was better remembered as manager of the famous downtown Town House.) The guests were dazzled by the velvet drapery, chandeliers glittering in many mirrors, and the sight of expensive murals.

They patronized the casino, of course, and enjoyed the combination dining room-dance floor. There was a bar room, separate from the cocktail lounge, and also a "Red Room," for which we have heard no explanation and leave it up to your speculation.

Although this columnist now qualifies as the newspaper's token Old-Timer, we cannot verify any of the above descriptions from personal observation. We did indeed enter the highfalutin' premises of the Country Club back in our mid-college days, but were quickly ejected by the greeter-bouncer on the grounds that "You college kids ain't allowed in here!" So, much of this report is made on hearsay a half-century later.

At the beginning, there were actually two house bands and a nightly broadcast from Reno's lone radio station, KOH. Counting musicians, the Country Club boasted 50 employees.

Despite all the fanfare and expensive trappings, the Country Club did not prosper at first. In fact, it was closed within a few weeks. But, refinanced by more of the "silent" Reno businessmen with the announcement that all debts had been paid up, the club re-opened within a few weeks under management of J.E. Merrill, who had replaced Charlie Rennie. Not only were the bills all paid, it was announced, but the club was now operating "in the black."

However, along came the fateful May 15, 1936. At 4 a.m. a night watchman discovered flames billowing from the kitchen area. The meager fire-fighting efforts were hopelessly inadequate. Since the Country Club on Plumas Street was then outside the Reno city limits, the county fire truck took the call. And two firemen vainly tried to quell the conflagration. Lacking any fire hydrant to tie into, they had to climb a fence rimming the adjoining Washoe County Golf Course (no connection with the country club) and go to an irrigation ditch for their water—200 yards away. Later, three Reno city firemen joined the hopeless battle. The gaudy Country Club was wiped out in two hours.

In addition to the club building and furnishings, there were other losses. The entertainers and musicians lost all their costumes and instruments. KOH's broadcasting setup was destroyed, too.

To help the Eddie Oliver Band and other employees, a benefit affair was held at the Riverside Hotel. Oliver's musicians played with instruments borrowed from Mariner's music store. Later, a benefit dance was held at Tony's El Patio Ballroom, with music by Merle Carlson's band from the Tavern night club.

There was a lot of speculation on the cause of the fire, but most evidence pointed to something happening in the kitchen. Insurance carried on the $225,000 layout was good for just $100,000.

Nevertheless, the management bravely announced plans for rebuilding. "A new structure will arise," they were quoted in the Reno newspapers. But that was as far as "rebuilding" got.

And now, 47 years later, a fragment of masonry, a piece of the fireplace and a few other ruins are still visible to Plumas Street passersby.

—November 27, 1983

Cobb's All-Star, all-time Silver Sox team
You can call 'em Padres now.

But for 33 previous seasons they were the Reno Silver Sox.

Since the "Silver Sox" name has been phased out in favor of the parent Padres, it gives us a chance to select an all-time Reno Silver Sox team.

Perhaps 33 years from now, some writer will announce his choices for "All-time Reno Padres team."

Having watched the local ball clubs since that opening day back in 1947 when Reno made its debut in professional baseball, we feel qualified to offer our "all-time" team. It's certain to raise some arguments, and perhaps we have left off deserving stars. Some players on previous Reno clubs blazed like meteors during their minor league stints, but never got to the big leagues. And others who looked inept and futureless while at Moana Park later blossomed as major league superstars. With mixed criteria for selections, we used our own feelings in some cases.

Let's take a look at these:

Designated Hitter—Fran Boniar. During that almost legendary season of 1957, he stroked an amazing .430 average, which is the California League all-time record. In Boniar's three minor league seasons (an injury kept him out of the majors) he twice won the Silver Bat for best average in all of baseball!

Pinch Hitter—for a sure batting eye and dependability, let's tab Lillio Marcucci, catcher and manager of the 1949 Sox. His .400 average led the Sunset League batsmen.

First Base—who can forget those tape-measure homers belted by Dick Nen in 1961, many of them landing far along the roof of the Moana swimming pool building? Nen led the Cal League in homers with 32, and in runs-batted-in with an amazing 144. He had six seasons, with the Dodgers, Cubs and Washington Senators.

Second Base—Duane Kuiper was one of the finest second basemen in the American League for a number of years, and he was team captain for Cleveland Indians as well as a steady hitter. He is always well up in All-Star balloting. He showed class with Reno, and moved up fast to the big leagues in 1974. A close pick behind Kuiper would be Jim LeFebvre, who had a long career with the Dodgers. (Kuiper is now with San Francisco Giants.)

Shortstop—Edging out Jack Heidemann and Donnie Williams is the durable Charlie Smith, a line-drive hitter for Reno back in the 1950s who became a much-traveled major leaguer. Smith, who now resides in Sparks, went up to the "Bigs" in 1960, with the Dodgers. Then he was with the Phillies, the Cubs, White Sox, New York Mets. He went to the Cardinals, to the Yankees (for Roger Maris) and wound up his 10th year in the majors with the Chicago Cubs.

Third Base—"Too big for a third baseman," they said of the strapping, 6-3, Ken McMullen when he broke in with Reno's pennant-winners of the early '60s. He went on to prove them wrong, and stayed in the majors for 18 years! He was with the Dodgers, Washington Senators, Angels, Milwaukee and finally Oakland, hitting nearly 170 homers in his long career.

Left Field—Gene Richards had the mark of greatness when he donned a Reno uniform in 1975, and he led the league in batting with .381, stolen bases with 85, and in other categories. Two years later he was burning up the National League basepaths, setting a (56) league record of stolen bases by a rookie. Since then he has consistently batted over .300 for San Diego, where he is considered the Padres' best all-around star.

Center Field—Willie Davis came to Reno in 1959 with a background as national high school champion sprinter and broad jumper. He burned up the Cal League, winning the batting title at .365, Rookie of Year and Most Valuable Player. One year later he moved into the majors with L.A. Dodgers and was a big leaguer through 1979. In his early two-score-year tenure, he was a Dodger for 13 years, then played with Texas, St. Louis and the Angels.

Right Field—Who hit the most homers as a Silver Sox? Jose Vidal did, that's who, 40 of them. That's a team record for Reno. The husky Dominican led the Cal loop in homers, in batting with .368, RBI's with a stunning 162, plus league MVP honors, all in 1963. He put in several seasons with Cleveland, then Seattle.

Catchers—Butch Wynegar not only burned up the Cal League in his Class A debut in Reno, but next season immediately jumped in a major league starting lineup, as catcher and cleanup batter! Wynegar helped Reno win the 1975 pennant, led the loop in RBI's, and next year became a permanent fixture with the Minnesota Twins. Reno has been blessed with great catchers over the years, such as Ray Fosse, Alan Ashby, Dan Graham, among others.

Pinch Runner—Tom "Hotfoot" Humber set a Cal League record of 75 stolen bases back in '57. Bobby Tolan went from Reno to become a major league leader in this department during his dozen years in the big leagues.

Pitchers—Any all-time Reno team must begin with Al Corwin, slick right-hander who won 28 games, including the playoffs, in the 1948 Sunset League. He was soon with New York and played a big role in the Giants' famous 1951 pennant drive.

One of the perennial pitching stars of the American League is Dennis Eckersley, ace of the Red Sox staff. Since breaking in with Cleveland in 1975, he has averaged 15 wins a season and twice has topped the 20-win mark, as well as making two All-Star games.

Dick Tidrow pitched parts of five different seasons with Reno. He eventually moved up to Cleveland in 1972, as a starter. Obtained by the Yankees, he was switched to relief pitching with great success, which has continued since he was acquired by Chicago Clubs and now Chicago White Sox. He has been around the top in ERA and saves.

Jim Kern, the 6-5 fastballer of the Texas Rangers and now Chicago White Sox, showed his budding talents with Reno before moving up to Cleveland Indians. When with Texas, he led the American League relievers in ERA, and has made two All-Star games.

Ed Farmer was good with Reno, went to the big leagues early, but bounced around between Cleveland, Detroit, Philadelphia, Milwaukee and Baltimore. He has reached the peaks with Chicago White Sox, leading the American League in "saves."

Slim southpaw Pete Richert totaled 80 victories in the big leagues after being groomed with Reno back in the 1950s. He broke in with the Dodgers of 1962, traveled to Washington and Baltimore. He won 15 and 14 with the lowly Senators, also played in one World Series with the Orioles.

Bill Singer the 6-4 righthander, was certainly durable. After a 15-win season with Reno in the early '60s, he later put in 14 years in the major leagues, mainly with Los Angeles Dodgers and Angels. His 118 total big league victories included two 20-win seasons, and a career total of 1,515 strikeouts.

Honorable mention, pitchers—Lefties Buzz Knudson, who totaled about 40 wins in 1948 and '49; and Bruce Gardner, 20-game winner in his lone season here.

Relief pitcher—the strong and ready arm of Rapid Robert Arrighi whose name is still enshrined in the Cal League record book for his 69 games pitched in relief in 1960.

Manager—OK, so he never won a pennant with Reno, but… Ray Perry is the all-time manager. For spirit, color, savvy, the "Little Buffalo" was probably the most popular Renoite of them all.

Coaches—They won pennants for Reno, so let's make our coaches—Roy Smalley, Tom Saffel and Harry Warner our honorary coaches.

Umpires—Let's not forget the arbiters. There have been many good ones, though you can't convince the fans. Doug Harvey and Bob Engle were a team more than 20 years ago, and have been outstanding in the major leagues ever since. —*September 25, 1983*

Jake Lawlor was noted for his intensity during games and a short-fused temper

The chief speaker at the Lawlor Events Center dedication luncheon recalled his first encounter with the fabled UNR coach for whom the new facility is named.

Jake Lawlor was noted for his intensity during games, as well as a short-fused temper.

"I was a high school sophomore at Las Vegas," explained the luncheon speaker, "and a student manager for basketball. When the Nevada Wolf Pack came to Las Vegas to play Loyola, it was in our gym. After the halftime intermission, Pat Diskin sent me to notify the Nevada coach and team to come back on the floor for the second half. I knocked timidly at the locker room door, but got no response as Coach Lawlor was still pointing out a few things to his team. So I opened the door and announced to Jake it was time to come out on the floor. The result was an angry explosion from Mr. Lawlor, who violently told me he would come out on the blankety-blank floor when he got good and ready, and to get out!"

The chastened prep sophomore who was given the verbal heave-ho from Jake Lawlor was Richard Bryan, who has since become governor of the state of Nevada. —*November 16, 1983*

He was a chubby little man with a ruddy face and rather long artistic-styled gray hair

The other day the names of famous actors were being discussed, and someone mentioned that of Gareth Hughes. And that mention brushed away a cobweb, and we recalled an amateur fight card at Wadsworth at least 30 years ago.

We had driven to Wadsworth to see the card staged by the Pyramid Lake Paiute Indians, whose boxers met several Reno scrappers. Among the latter were Robert "Frenchy" Laxalt, Moe Macias and Jack Swobe.

We didn't pay much attention to the ring announcer climbing through the ropes, only to note he was a chubby little man with a ruddy face and rather long artistic-styled gray hair. But when he spoke, we perked up. Never had we heard a fight announcer speaking in polished, cultured tones. The trained voice of an actor, a Broadway theater voice, and not quite what you'd expect to hear in a small Nevada town.

"Who's that?" we asked an Indian friend. "Oh, that's Brother David," he replied, leaving us as mystified as ever.

We noted that the fans treated the little gentleman with friendly respect. We finally found out he was the pastor of the Indian church at Nixon. But it was not until later we learned his real name was Gareth Hughes, and that he had a great reputation in New York and London as a Shakespearean actor. He had also played roles in the movies, and during his years at Pyramid Lake he was frequently visited by famous Hollywood figures. Gareth Hughes, at the peak of his thespian career, had switched to a religious life, abandoned the theater and devoted himself to religious work among the Nevada Indians. Ill health eventually ended this career and he died a few years later.

We wondered if Bob Laxalt remembered that startling "fight announcer" at the Wadsworth card. "I sure do," he reminisced. "I was sitting in my corner in the ring really nervous and waiting for the first gong. Then I heard that extraordinary voice, so trained and cultured, announcing my name and weight. I almost fell off the stool."

Brother David put as much zest into his fight card announcing as he did in his religious work. He's still missed by the Native Nevadans of Pyramid Lake. —*January 7, 1981*

The King of Horses appeared on the track, with his rider up in his winning colors

Who was the greatest champion ever produced in Nevada? You can get an argument no matter how you answer that one. But not many could outtalk you if you offered the name of native-born El Rio Rey.

Back in the 1880s, El Rio Rey was born in Washoe Valley in a stable on the lush ranch owned by Theodore Winters adjoining the shores of Washoe Lake. Some of the Winters ranch still remains, though the gigantic barn is getting saggy, and the once elaborate mansion is "not what it used to be." Motorists hurrying to and from Carson City seldom give the old home a second glance. About a century ago Winters (whose first name was always abbreviated "Theo," in the newspapers) established his holdings in the valley, only a few miles from where Sandy Bowers built his fabulous mansion.

Theo Winters developed a string of outstanding race horses, who flourished on the sandy-bottom meadow. The gem of the stable was El Rio Rey. He had fantastic speed, at a half or three-quarters of a mile. Winters took him to the Midwest and Eastern tracks. At St. Louis, Chicago and on New York tracks the sleek Nevada-bred racer amazed the railbirds. He set records in race after race and for years his time of 1:11 for the three-quarters was the world's fastest.

Winters refused offers to sell the young horse, for sums which were almost unheard of in that day. Even after an untimely illness affected El Rio Rey, forcing his retirement while still a two-year-old, Winters received and turned down substantial offers. He brought El Rio Rey home to Washoe Valley and while other Winters horses, notably Yo Tambien, made reputations on Eastern tracks, El Rio Rey (The River King) remained the showpiece of the ranch.

A few years later the king returned to the turf, for an exhibition romp around the race track at the State Fair in Reno. An overflowing crowd of more than 5,000 Nevadans jammed the stands on that sunny September day in 1891.

The *Nevada State Journal* quoted its former publisher, Gen. C. C. Powning, who made a speech introducing El Rio Rey. The General (he got the title from serving as state surveyor general) was an official of the Nevada Agricultural Society which staged the fair, and from the bunting-covered platform he spoke:

"El Rio Rey is Nevada's pride. He is the sixth son of Norfolk and Marion. He started in races against the best horses in the world and was never beaten. He has the best three-quarters time of a two-year-old … He is the winner of $80,000 in purses for his owner, who refused to sell him, before his illness, for $50,000."

The *Journal* reporter described the exhibition run of the old champion: "The King of Horses appeared on the track, with his rider up in *his* winning colors. This was the signal for a wild burst of applause, in which the ladies joined. The noble and beautiful animal seemed to appreciate the compliment, bowing his head several times, and his rider felt that he was a bigger man than the President… The horse was galloped around the track in his beautiful, flowing stride, and he came down the home stretch at full speed. Men cheered, ladies waved their handkerchiefs and the band played 'Hail to the Chief' as the King of Horses gracefully swept up the track and passed under the wire. A wreath of roses was placed on his neck by Miss Mamie Bell, and the intelligent animal pranced proudly to his stable." —*Sept. 19, 1971*

Our favorite diversion was to sit beneath the Paterson's kitchen window and listen to Mildred sing and whistle

Sometimes, when a story seems far-fetched or unbelievable, skeptics call it a "crock." Well, this item is not really "a crock," but it is actually all about a crock.

Not long ago, we were attending a delightful reception honoring Dorothy and Hal Rohlfing, who were celebrating their 50th wedding anniversary.

And many friends of many years were present, renewing old acquaintances.

Among those we greeted were Mr. and Mrs. William Paterson, Sr.

While the debonair clothing store founder Bill Paterson was drifting around, socializing, we chatted with Mildred Paterson.

Socko! An imaginary tussle with Archie Moore, world light-heavy weight champion. Paul Laxalt, governor and U.S. Senator, is the referee.

We spoke of the day in the late 1920s when we lived in the same neighborhood in Reno's Burke's Addition, the Patersons on East Taylor and the Cobbs on Wheeler Avenue. Bill Paterson, Jr. was one of our buddies (younger brother Jim was a comparative toddler). And our favorite diversion was to sit beneath the Patersons' kitchen window and listen to Mildred sing and whistle. This lovely woman had a fine singing voice, but she was most proficient at whistling.

When she puckered up and trilled, it was like hearing a musical instrument. Classical tunes, popular songs, Mildred was the finest whistler we ever heard. They even had her on the radio, on Reno's lone station KOH.

Well, we talked of the days of her whistling and other topics, and then Mildred Paterson asked: "Did I ever tell you about your uncle Bill and my stone crock?"

This was a new one. "Uncle Bill" was William S. Harris, who was employed for nearly two decades as clerk of the Nevada State Prison.

He handled all the slammer's books, correspondence and other paper-work. As an official assistant warden, he had other duties, too. On one occasion—this was probably in the late 1930s—he telephoned Mrs. Paterson. "Mildred," he implored, "I've been looking all over Carson and Reno, high and low, for a big stone crock. We need one badly. One of those thick stone jars about two feet high. Can't find one anywhere. I hear you have a good one. Can I use it?"

"Well," Mildred Paterson reminisced, "I told him that sure, he could use it. So he came over and took it."

For what purpose, she wasn't informed. She presumed that Uncle Bill Harris was going to make some homemade wine, or root beer, or such in the big old stone crock.

Later she found out.

"They were going to execute some convict at the prison, a con-demned murderer, and they needed my stone crock."

The State of Nevada occasionally executes criminals by the lethal gas method. The condemned killer is secured in the gas chamber, a small air-tight room. Someone pulls a lever and a couple of "eggs" (cyanide pellets) are dropped into a container—the stone crock. In-stantly the poison gas is created and knocks off the felon.

"Anyway, that's what they used my stone crock for," Mrs. Paterson discovered.

"You know, they never returned that crock to me—and I never asked for it." —*February 17, 1981*

Players were subjected to such harassment as pinching, or even more indelicate indignities

Of course, you've heard of "The Mark of Zorro." But how about "The Mark of Lawlor?"

Jake Lawlor wasn't a masked swordsman of California fictions. He was a tough basketball player of Virginia City fame. When the fa-mous athlete-coach-etc. died in Reno last July, he was hailed as a leg-end in his own time. His exploits and traits were topics revived by the hundreds of Nevadans who mourned his loss. Not the least of these Lawlorisms was the *"Brand of the Big Stove."*

To explain this phenomenon, we must give some background.

In the 1930s, when Jake Lawlor coached at Virginia City, and for some years before and after his regime, Comstock teams played basketball in the old National Guard Hall. This was an imposing stone structure on "C" Street, the main drag of the old mining camp, and it served as the social center of the mountainside community. It was about three stories in front, and, being built on a steep hillside, was about five floors high on the back end of "D" Street. It had been used in the old days as an armory for the National Guard. (There were several rival militia companies during the hey-day of the Comstock Lode.) Long after the Guard ceased to exist, the big hall was used for movies, grand balls, boxing cards, political rallies, graduations, and other functions. But its main use was for *basketball.*

One entered the National Guard Hall by descending a roofed-over flight of stairs from the main street to the lobby floor. Here was the ticket office, and entry to seating of the large balcony which overhung the auditorium's main room. A double flight of stairs led down to the entry lobby and dressing rooms, and the swinging doors to the main room.

It was a fair-sized arena, as far as playing space went, but there was barely room for a single line of chairs on either side. The balcony hung over the west end, while the east end terminated abruptly at a stage. This was used for school plays, public speakers, orchestras and other purposes. But in the winters, it supported the basketball backboard.

These dimensions *did* curtail some of the action, which was tailored to fit the arena. Players driving for the east basket were obliged to pull up quickly or else crash into the stage. But those heading west, where the basket backboard hung from the balcony overhang, could "go all the way." They could drive in for a layup and continue their momentum on for some distance, even through the swinging door to the entry lobby.

This called for some localized strategy and the home teams were particularly adept at halting in front of the stage or following-through past the other basket. Visiting players often complained that the locals had given them a rough ride into the projecting stage, or that some spectators in the sideline chairs had tripped them. Or, when throwing the ball in bounds from the narrow sideline, sticking their posteriors in spectators' faces, they were subjected to such harassment as pinching, or even more indelicate indignities.

Jake Lawlor was often accused (not to his face) of fostering some of the rough tactics among the cagers he coached at the high school, but these were insignificant in comparison to the episodes of the hot stove.

We did not mention that the National Guard Hall auditorium was a lofty one. The ceilings were way up there, so high they'd equal three floors of a modern building. (The playing floor was easy on the feet, and was reputed to have been mounted on massive "railroad springs" which gave it a bouncy effect.) The plaster ceilings were smoke-stained but hardly cracked. Never cracked until, during one game in the end of the 1930s decade, a huge chunk of eight-inch-thick plaster came crashing down to the basketball court. The game was called as more plaster started to plop down.

It was the last ever played at old National Guard Hall. During the night great cracks began to open throughout the building, and part of the rear end on "D" Street came toppling down in a roar of stone and plaster. There were a few business offices upstairs, as well as the weekly newspaper's one-room plant. These were abruptly vacated, and demolition crews soon pulled down the picturesque but doomed old facility.

But—back to the famous stove, and the main topic of our story: the entire hall was heated by just one stove. This was a huge barrel-like coal burner located at the southeast corner (next to the stage) of the great room. It took a lot of coal to keep that ol' stove roaring and its sides often glowed red-hot after several hours of fueling.

This writer had a personal acquaintance with the famous stove, probably more than any other person of that time.

We held a part-time (very) job as student janitor of the basketball hall, sometimes sharing this distinction with our friend Dan Connors, Jr. Since the girls team practice began around 4:30 p.m., we'd leave the Fourth Ward School earlier in the late afternoon and trudge downtown to the National Guard Hall. There we'd start a fire in the big stove and in smaller stoves which warmed the dressing rooms and heated shower water.

The big stove was not easy to get going. Often a balky draft would play havoc with the new flame and send great billows of smoke ceiling-ward. Sometimes coach Jake Lawlor or principal John Gilmartin would arrive, sniff the heavy aroma of errant smoke, gaze at the smoke-blackened ceiling and direct unkind remarks at the culprit student janitors.

Nevertheless, we usually got the stove working well, and particularly on Fridays and Saturdays when there was an array of games. Basketball was big on the Comstock in those depression years when there was scant recreation for anyone. The junior varsity game would start off the program, to be followed by the girls competition. Then would come the main high school varsity contest. The main event, however, was the fourth tilt of the evening—the *"town team"* classic.

Sponsored by the Comstock Earie of Eagles, the Virginia townies had a powerhouse. These miners and teachers were veteran players and built imposing records. They often played the University of Nevada varsity, and once came within one point of the Wolf Pack.

We recall such as Merve and Neil (Doc) Gallagher, Tex Gladding, Del Benner, Jack Flanagan, John Gilmartin and others. Particularly *Jake Lawlor.*

Some people could not picture the hefty Lawlor as a basketball player, noting his huge bulk on a not-so-tall frame. His build was deceptive. He could move like a cat, spot action with his uncanny side vision, and he loved *contact.* His ruddy-faced scowl was often illuminated by a benign smile after a particularly hard collision with an opposing cager.

Opponents learned to give him all the space he wanted, after being driven into the ledge projecting from the stage. Or being crashed by the 240-pound Jake and somehow being flung against the Big Stove.

It was like a scene from a branding corral, said one opponent from an agricultural community. "The scent of seared flesh was reminiscent of that left by a branding iron on a calf's hide."

For years numerous ex-athletes would bring up this subject. Jake always vigorously denied he ever *knowingly* had jolted any victim onto that hot stove. But with an unconvincing smirk. He even pointed out that he had—a considerable time later—some guard rails installed around the offending stove.

The National Guard Hall is long gone now—it caved in more than 40 years ago. And Jake Lawlor is gone, too, but his legend lives on.

There are any number of middle-aged (or old) men around Nevada who'll tell you that under their trousers they still carry, today, the *"Mark of Lawlor." —April 5, 1981*

Three or four unscrupulous characters decided to jump the claim

The story of a mining camp confrontation, the most famous gun-fighter of them all, and the lad who imitated him via hero-worship. That was the yarn retold the other day at a Reno funeral service.

This concerns two "old timers" who were kids together in Tonopah in its earliest days. One of them died in Reno a few days ago. That was Jack Lindsay, well known for his career involving veterans affairs in Nevada. At his memorial service, his eulogy was delivered by his life-time friend, retired Navy captain Jack Howell.

As Howell recalled, there was a choice piece of potential mining property on the boundary line between a couple of the early-day major mines of Tonopah. Apparently, it belonged to Jim Butler, the almost-legendary discoverer of Tonopah's rich minerals, and thereby also to his business partner Tasker Oddie, then a young lawyer (who later became Nevada governor).

Three or four unscrupulous characters decided to jump the claim. Howell recalls that, according to mining law, people trying to take possession of a claim had one full day to dig a hole three feet deep and a much wider distance across.

"Tasker Oddie—a slim, quiet, bald-headed young man, went over to where this gang was digging," says Jack Howell. "He informed them they were digging on Jim Butler's land and ordered them to stop work." They coolly informed the young attorney that he should leave them alone and get out of there. He looked at the tough fellows' array of guns and complied with their request.

Then Oddie suggested that the sheriff take over the cease-and-desist affair. But the sheriff, too, was intimidated by the display of weapons and threats, says Howell, and the lawman also went away promptly.

Wyatt Earp was a sort of deputy, and also security man for some of the big mining interests, so the famous gunfighter-lawman thought he'd check into the affair. "He wore a stylish felt hat, a dark suit with a vest which displayed a huge gold watch chain across the chest," recalls Howell, who was an acquaintance of Earp. "He had a habit of hooking his thumbs into his vest pockets, just below the big watch chain."

Earp informed the claim-jumpers they were trespassing on the property of Jim Butler. And who did he think he was? sneered the tough quartet.

"I'm Wyatt Earp," responded the notorious quickdraw expert—who wasn't even packing a Colt .45 that day.

"Yes, sir, Mr. Earp," chorused the would-be claim-jumpers, "We'll get out of here."

At Earp's cold suggestion, they hastened to fill up the hole they had dug. "Good," observed the famous hero of the OK Corral and other gunfights. "Now I suggest that you get off this property quick. In fact, I think you'd better get out of Tonopah quick-like. And while you're at it, get out of the country, too."

They got.

Wyatt Earp came up to Jack Howell's father's house for dinner that night.

"And several other times, too. Jack Lindsay and us other kids always stood by the gate to look at him, and exchange hellos. Jack Lindsay was the most impressed. Years later I noticed that Jack always wore a dark suit just like Wyatt Earp's, the same kind of felt hat, and even a big gold watch chain across the vest." Lindsay even hooked his thumbs in his vest pockets, just like his boyhood hero Earp did.

—June 7, 1981

Bachelors of a jolly nature flocked there for the dances, the horse racing, and to engage in land squabbles

Before the arrival in 1858 of Granville Huffaker driving 500 head of cattle, the principal settlers in the Truckee Meadows were the early Mormon farmers. It would be a year later before the mines of the Comstock Lode were first developed; and Huffaker established his permanent ranch the same year, 1859. Almost immediately, Huffaker's ranch became a center of activity in the lush valley. Reno was a sparse settlement of a few shacks—and didn't become an official townsite until 1868.

At or near the Huffaker ranch, Langston's Stage Line established a stage coach stop. The first U.S. post office in the area was functioning there by 1862. The Huffaker school house was constructed there in 1868, to serve the growing families of the southwest Truckee Meadows settlers.

Huffaker's spacious ranch house was the social center of the area. An old-time writer said that "Bachelors of a jolly nature flocked there for the dances, the horse racing, and to engage in land squabbles." The Athenian Literary Society flourished there "for the cultured."

In booming Virginia City, the Bonanza Kings (Mackay, Fair, Flood and O'Brien) were reaping harvests of gold and silver from their great mines. And to meet the incessant demand for more lumber to shore up their shafts, tunnels and stopes, they established the Pacific Lumber and Flume Company. This was established to facilitate shipment of lumber from the great forests around Lake Tahoe. The logs were taken from the Tahoe basin, sometimes towed across the wide lake, hauled to the mountain ridges above Crystal Bay and propelled down the eastern slope into the Truckee Meadows.

The huge logs rumbled down the 15 miles of trough-like flumes to the valley floor, most of them terminating near the Huffaker ranch house. Near this terminus of the flume, the Virginia & Truckee Railroad was already running a north-south line between Reno and Carson City (thence to Virginia City). The V&T ran a spur track to Huffaker's where the big logs were deposited. A depot and telegraph office also were established. For many years, the Huffaker ranch continued to be a center for business and social life in its area.

After the death in 1905 of Sam Huffaker, cousin of the late Granville Huffaker, the main house was occupied by Mr. and Mrs. Thad Holcomb. Thad was the son of George Holcomb, one of Nevada's most prominent ranchers. The Holcomb estates purchased the Huffaker land, and was the valley's largest owner of that time.

All this historical background leads up to an event scheduled for next Saturday, Nov. 14, at the site of the Huffaker ranch house. (Near South Virginia Street or 395 South, between Holcomb and Foothill lanes.)

A historical landmark will be dedicated on the site, with the heritage-minded Daughters of American Colonists as the chief instigators. A public dedication ceremony will be held with Bill Swackhamer, Nevada's secretary of state. The Huffaker descendants, as well as those of other native sons and daughters of the early settlers will be introduced. There will be reminisces made by Janet Holcomb Hunter, and "school days" by Rose Bullis. There will be V&T railroad recollections by Bill Norton, and remarks by Mimi Rodden (Nevada state director of historical preservation) and a tribute to the pioneers by Swackhamer. There will be more to the program followed by a reception at the Huffaker school.

One of the stories which is certain to be detailed during the program is that of the wild ride down the logging trestle in the 1870s. Two visiting newsmen from the East Coast had been spending several days in Virginia City, chronicling the exploits of the Bonanza Kings and their enterprises. It was while showing the distinguished visitors the Tahoe logging operations that one of the silver kings got the bright idea of giving them a ride down the trestle. Instead of the huge logs, two skinny boats, which "resembled pig troughs" were provided. Each of the mining monarchs reposed in a boat, along with each of the visiting writers. Borne by the torrent of water, they "were off and running."

A colorful, illustrated account of the wild ride was printed in an Eastern publication, and has frequently been re-printed locally. The terrified riders were borne down the trestle at break-neck speed—

"swifter than any railroad train could go." They finally splashed into the log pond at the valley floor end of the flume, at Huffaker's, dazed and drenched. It was noted that the Bonanza Kings, risking their necks to provide their visitors a first-hand thrill, were worth about $30 million, a valuable cargo for a reckless ride—which was never repeated!

—*November 8, 1981*

The three-day fete included live-pigeon shoots, a horse race, and other prize fights

The recent Leonard-Finch fight in Reno revived interest in previous world championship bouts held in Northern Nevada.

It focused attention on the first world title fight in this area, the Corbett-Fitzsimmons scrap for the heavyweight championship on March 17, 1897.

That was held in Carson City, but the passage of the years—85 of them—and the growth of the capital city literally obliterated memory of the site of the historic fight arena. Although the attention of the sporting world was focused on Carson at the time that Bob Fitzsimmons KO'd champion Jim Corbett, few details of the arrangements have been preserved.

Information on the fight itself is plentiful, but less was known about the special outdoor arena built for the fight; and the site was generally forgotten for many decades.

Now it has been located!

Through the efforts of Nevada historians, definite proof of the location of the arena has been documented.

It was through the work of these dedicated historians that the Reno site of the 1910 fight between Jim Jeffries and Jack Johnson was verified, and a large marker was erected at the locale. That was only two years ago and Yours Truly was the speaker at the ceremony at East Fourth and Toano streets. Phillip Earl, master of ceremonies, introduced a special guest, the daughter of promoter Tex Rickard, who had flown from Florida to attend.

Now, a similar dedication ceremony will be conducted in Carson City soon.

Several people took part in the tedious research of the locale, and Guy Louis Rocha, Nevada state archivist, said that even the assessment rolls for 1897 were studied. The Nevada Landmark Society of Carson City and Nevada State Division of Archives, joined in this research, and together will sponsor dedication of "Historical Marker 243."

It's at the corner of Pratt and Musser streets, at the entrance of the Sheriff's Office Building.

The dedication ceremony will be at 2 p.m., March 14, with the public invited.

This date is only three days before the 85th anniversary of the famous fight on St. Patrick's Day, 1897.

"Gentleman Jim" Corbett was the reigning heavyweight champion, having taken that title from the legendary John L. Sullivan (in New Orleans, 21st round) in 1892. Sullivan had been recognized as first champion under the "modern" Marquis of Queensbury rules, which called for the use of gloves by the fighters, and timed rounds. (In previous times, a round ended only when one of the fighters went down, either voluntarily to gain a rest, or from a blow. The last round of the Sullivan-Mitchell fight in 1888 lasted 35 minutes.)

Corbett only defended his crown once in the five years before the Carson City bout, knocking out England's Charlie Mitchell.

The Nevada Legislature cooperated with promoter Dan Stuart in clearing the way for the Fitzsimmons-Corbett fight, legalizing this "fight to the finish." (Johnson-Jeffries, 13 years later in Reno, was scheduled for *only* 45 rounds!)

The Carson & Tahoe Flume & Lumber Co., of which the noted D.L. Bliss of Glenbrook was president, furnished lumber for building of the arena. This writer has possession of the official fight program, six by eight inches in size, and 50 pages in length. It includes a map of the arena, as rendered by P.J. Donovan, architect and builder.

These were the ticket prices: three back rows of the outer circle, $5; general admission, $10; reserved seats, $20; numbered box seats, $40. Terms of the fight included: a $15,000 purse for the winner; $5,000 deposit to be posted by the promoter.

At the Tahoe City golf course in a foursome with, l-r, young golf pro Tommy Jacobs, gambler Charlie Resnick, and Bob Hope—note his right hand.

The program was well filled with advertisements, chiefly from San Francisco saloons and race tracks, and illustrated with photos of the promoter, referee George Siler, and various "sportsmen." Also biographies of Corbett and Fitzsimmons, and pictures of other fighters appearing in "Dan Stuart's Fistic Carnival." It was a three-day fete including live-pigeon shoots, a horse race, and other prize fights.

The promoter kindly reserved a ringside section for the ladies, surrounded in canvas to shield the fair sex from the gawks of the male spectators. And there was a special stand for the movie cameramen. This was the first major fight to be recorded on the new-fangled motion picture machine.

It was also notable for drawing nationwide press coverage, headed by the enterprising *San Francisco Examiner* which sent a special train to the site. Immediately after the fight ended, the *Examiner* staff rushed to the "special," on the Virginia & Truckee tracks, thence to Reno where it was switched to the Southern Pacific and given "highball" clearance as it roared toward San Francisco. Meanwhile, the writers completed their stories and the photographers developed their glass negatives in a special darkroom car.

There was a break in the weather, which was fair as the fighters trained at their respective camps, one near Shaw's Hot Springs and the other near the prison. Fitzsimmons was badgered into an exhibition against a wrestler (a mixed match which generally has bad results for the boxer) and his powerful left hook sent the wrestler into dreamland in a few seconds!

Corbett reigned as favorite. After all, he had vanquished the "invincible" John L. Sullivan, and at 183 pounds had a good weight edge over the skinny Fitzsimmons. Handsome "Pompadour Jim"—so called for his hair style was regarded as a superb scientific boxer with a long record of victories.

Fitz was the lightest of all heavyweights, a mere 167 pounds on a 5-11 frame. However, the baldish, freckled native of Cornwall, England, had developed a mighty pair of shoulders in his youth as a blacksmith in New Zealand, and he packed a tremendous punch in either hand.

Actually, Fitzsimmons and Corbett had been signed to fight for the title two years previous, near Dallas, Texas, but were prevented by the police.

This writer received many first-hand accounts, as a teenager, of the Carson fight. Our next-door neighbor was elderly Dan Connors, one-time bare-knuckle fighter, boxing "professor," and correspondent for New York papers. He designed and sold quaint booklets in which the fighters were sketched in fighting pose, each page representing a round, with arrows designating the outstanding punches of the round. (While demonstrating Corbett's powerful jabs which split open Fitz' lip, Mr. Conners dealt us a resounding smack on the jaw!)

Corbett was apparently in command for the first dozen rounds, using his expert jab to slice up Ruby Robert's features. But Fitzsimmons began to score heavily, and in the 14th round he hurt the champ with a crunching blow to the neck. Then came a powerful left to the stomach.

Corbett's knees "turned to jelly" and he sagged to the canvas, writhing in pain. He staggered to his feet just after referee Siler tolled the final second—"ten and out!" (The sportswriters created the name "solar plexis punch" for this KO blow.)

Frustrated and angered, the defeated Corbett made a rush at Fitzsimmons, but it was too late, and he was fended off by the Cornishman's entourage.

Two years later Fitz lost his title to the bruiser, Jim Jeffries, who used his 40-pound weight edge to wear out the lanky old veteran.

We congratulate the Carson City historians for their diligence in rediscovering the site of Nevada's first world championship fight, and marking it permanently with this historical marker for all present and future generations to take note of. —*February 28, 1982*

Destroyers then closed in to sink the Nevada with gunfire

The super-dreadnought USS Nevada, which the Reno Council of the Navy League is planning, with assistance from the Nevada State Museum, to memorialize with a museum dedicated solely to its history and accomplishments, had to be the toughest warship ever tested.

At the end of World War II, after a short stay in Tokyo Bay, the Nevada was returned to Pearl Harbor for an "inspection and survey." It was determined that her age—32 years—and past damages rendered her incapable of further warlike service expected of a modern navy.

She was selected to be the "target ship" for "Operation Crossroads," which would test the effect of an atomic bomb.

Taken to Bikini Atoll in the Marshall Islands, the Nevada was anchored in the center of the nine-square mile lagoon. With her decks painted a bright orange, she became the target ship for the air-drop A-Bomb.

On June 30, 1946, a B-29 bomber from Kwajalein Atoll passed over the assembled ships at Bikini and dropped the missile.

In minutes the sea was a holocaust of flame and smoke, as the huge mushroom of water rose into the air, hiding the target from observation.

But when smoke and spray subsided, there was Nevada—riding majestically at anchor.

Another test was completed—an underwater explosion which also should have sunk the big ship, but didn't.

The Nevada was then towed back to Pearl Harbor where it was determined that while she still floated, her sides and superstructure had been hopelessly damaged and buckled. Because of the lingering radioactivity of the atomic tests, "she should be disposed by sinking."

The battleship was decommissioned Aug. 29, 1946. As the target ship of the task force, Nevada was towed to a point 65 miles southwest of Pearl Harbor. The Navy placed a secret explosive on board, and detonated it on July 26, 1948. The ship's side plates and decks buckled, three holes opening up in her old hull, and she settled slightly.

But remained afloat.

Destroyers then closed in to sink the Nevada with gunfire, and she rocked and pitched as salvo after salvo from the "tin cans" racked her from stem to stern.

But old Nevada remained defiantly afloat.

Next, the Navy called upon rocket firing-planes to end Nevada's agony. They covered the ship's superstructure and hull with hundreds of gashes.

But again she rebelled—and stayed afloat.

The mighty newer battleship Iowa was 10 miles away from the battered but unsinkable Nevada. She was ordered to fire her 16-inch guns with salvos against the Nevada, and soon the "target" was shrouded in smoke and spray, from the battleship's main batteries.

But when a gentle breeze cleared the smoke—there was USS Nevada, her decks riding high above the Pacific's waves!

Then three cruisers, Astoria, Pasadena and Springfield, were called in to send the Nevada to the bottom. They moved in close and hammered her with five and six-inch guns.

Only to leave Nevada still in her defiantly-floating position!

Navy dive bombers clobbered the target ship, to no avail. So torpedo bombers were called in. And shortly after 2 p.m., an aerial torpedo caught the Nevada amidships. She began listing slightly. Half an hour later the great ship sank in 2,600 fathoms of water. It was July 31, the fifth day of absorbing all the punishment the Navy could muster.

USS Nevada (BE-36, for the 36th state) has been awarded seven battle stars and other awards including Service Medal for operations at Pearl Harbor, the Aleutians, invasion of Normandy, invasion of southern France, the assault and occupation of Iwo Jima, the assault and occupation of Okinawa, Third Fleet operations against Japan.

What Nevadan can read this account of the gallant and unsinkable old battleship, which bore the name of this state, and fail to be thrilled.

—*June 6, 1982*

The old gals gratefully accepted their dash of sherry and expressed hope that the first bartender would not return

Evershaw's Tavern was the saloon on East Second Street, a short distance from the northeast corner of Second and Center streets. Parker's Western Clothing store was on the corner, and Evershaw's was next to it. Both are long gone, and the site is part of Harrah's parking lot.

In its time, chiefly the 1930s and '40s, Evershaw's Tavern was a hangout for many Renoites, including the swingers who were called "rounders" then. It was operated by Jack and Eleanor Evershaw. Jack was a huge man, portly, and wheezing from the effort of tilting his bulk on some bad legs. But he was tough and capable of handling boisterous and unruly patrons who got out of line. Evershaw's main adversaries, however, were the game wardens who differed on his own counts of game limits, such as "too many" ducks, geese, pheasant or other fowl. Eleanor Evershaw was a calmer personality who had a more tactful way of coping with tavern problems.

Evershaw's Tavern was a long and narrow layout, with a staff of pleasant ladies who chatted with the customers and entertained them musically. There was no cabaret then, such as is now levied on bars.

In the back was an elevated alcove where jovial Jackie Sherman presided at the piano, and a microphone from which Sadie (Basta) Shipley warbled. There were other singers, too, Marge, Pat and others whose names we can't recall now. Frank Sullivan, ex-Journal editor (the Journal newsroom was once located directly across the street from Evershaw's) remembers a hefty trio called "Three Tons of Harmony."

There were innumerable small saloons in the vicinity then. On the Center Street side of that block were the Silver Dollar, Ship 'n Bottle, Inferno, Overland and sometimes a couple more. But Evershaw's had a distinctive atmosphere. The bartenders included the witty Bruce Sheehy and the flamboyant Ray "Rinso" White. Their antics made a simple purchase of a glass of beer an adventure. One time three elderly ladies, tourists from Boston visiting Reno, wandered into Evershaw's for a touch of sherry.

Donning a Groucho Marx false mustache-nose-glasses disguise, and stuffing a pillow under his white jacket, "Rinso" White approached the timid trio with a gruff query: "Are you old bags back again? I thought we kicked you out last night. Do you want more of our rotgut whiskey again?" Before the shocked and scared elderly ladies could leave, White hastened to the store room, shucked his disguise and returned. Speaking smoothly and politely, he apologized for the rough demeanor of "his partner, who was crude and rude when he had been drinking."

Pacified and soothed by their urbane benefactor, the old gals gratefully accepted their dash of sherry and expressed the hope that the first bartender would not return.

One of the regular patrons of Evershaw's had an unfortunate experience which resulted in being tagged with a lifetime nickname. In a restroom mishap, he got part of his anatomy caught in his zipper. All the sympathetic efforts of the Evershaw's Tavern staff couldn't get him unzipped, and they toted him away to the hospital where he was painfully separated from the entangling facility. From that day on, no one knew the victim had a first name; he was forever known as "Zip."

132   TY COBB

There are other episodes from Evershaw's Tavern which we are unable to print in this, a family newspaper. But Eleanor Evershaw, widow of the cantankerous Jack Evershaw, enjoyed re-telling them again before her passing a few days ago. They were part of a colorful era now long gone. —*July 1, 1982*

The armed robbers waited until there were no customers present, then confronted Mr. Henley with wicked-looking pistols

In Virginia City, they're building a new bank. The Reno-based Valley Bank system is constructing a new building a few blocks below the main ("C") street, at the intersection of Union and "E" streets, right where the V&T railroad tunnel began. Or ended.

Now, banking institutions on the fabulous Comstock Lode are nothing new, Back in the boom days, in the 1860-80 era, the Bank of California had its most lively branch in Virginia City. It was directed by Sharon, arch-rival of Bonanza Kings Mackay and Fair; he later became U.S. Senator from the new state of Nevada.

When we say "nothing new" we speak

> **BUS PROBLEMS**
>
> *It seems that just about every bus in the country has a sign in the window, advising its destination, or who is chartering it, etc. Not so the big vehicle sighted in Susanville. The sign said, "Wrong Bus."*
> —*April 23, 1978*

in broad terms. The Comstock Lode has not had a bank for more than a half century. And therein lies our story of how a misdemeanor foiled a major felony.

Guess we'd better explain this in chronological order:

The last bank to exist in Virginia City served the Comstock people until it became a victim of the Great Depression, which was felt in Nevada first in the 1929-30 era. It was also the victim of the last bank robbery in Virginia City, about 52 years ago. The Virginia City bank was virtually a one-man operation, with William Henley, Sr., as practically the whole staff—manager, loan officer, teller, etc.

Two schemers decided to hit the Virginia bank, and after scouting out the situation, made their move. They had parked their car less than 200 yards away on "D" Street, just a short distance down Taylor Street from the bank. The bank was located on "C" Street, near the corner of Taylor, in a site later occupied for many years by the Sazarec Saloon.

The armed robbers waited until there were no customers present, then confronted Mr. Henley with wicked-looking pistols. They tied him up with ropes, and deposited their victim on the floor, behind the counter. Unable to open the vault, which apparently had a time lock, they scooped up all the currency and cash from the drawers—and fled.

Just moments later, the trussed-up Bill Henley, Sr., was discovered. The alarm was given and pursuit began. Lawmen, quick on the trail of the fugitives, chased them down the Six-Mile Canyon, but the bandits seemed well on the way to a successful escape, as they roared across the dusty desert road past Sutro. Then, their getaway car ran out of gas!

The bank robbers tried to flee on foot, but were captured. Tried. And sentenced to prison. Some, but not all, of the loot was discovered.

We discussed this adventure recently with a man who spent most of his life in Virginia City, and who was a boy when the Great Bank Robbery took place. After a few moments discussion, he asked, "Do you know why those bandits' car ran out of gas so soon?"

"No idea."

"Well, it was because we—my two young friends and I—had siphoned the gasoline out of their car's tank."

One of the sub-teen kids owned an auto, sort of. It was a "Bus," a stripped-down Model T which was without a body, fenders or other frills. Just a frame and engine which ran noisily, whenever the youthful motorists could provide a bit of gasoline.

Our friend seemed rather embarrassed, even a half-century later, at admitting to swiping gasoline out of some strangers' car. But their prank actually was the means of thwarting a daring bank robbery.

"That was more than 50 years ago; why didn't you ever say anything about it in all that time?" we queried.

"Well, we were afraid to say anything about it. We were scared the robbers, when they got out of prison, would come after us for revenge."

So, with a newsman's heeding of the old standard of keeping a sacred trust and never revealing his sources, we will keep the faith. And won't reveal the identity of three small boys who swiped gasoline out of the robbers' car. And thwarted the getaway of the bandits.

Even though those bandits, if not dead by now, or still in prison, must be in their 80s and not very revenge-minded by this time!

—July 11, 1982

It was no mean feat to trundle the heavy barrow across the steaming, slippery and very hot ovens

"Sweeping Away the Cobbwebs" was the original title of this column, but today we're going to tell you about *sweeping away the money.* Or, at least, *sweeping it up.*

Back in the late '30s, we were fortunate to land a job with the Arizona-Comstock Mining Company, which had acquired the site of the former Hale-Norcross Mine (several hundred yards below the Fourth Ward School). Then it constructed a mill some distance below the mine tunnel, by coincidence, on the site of a house where this writer was born.

This teenager became a "handy man" around the mill, with chief duties of tending to and building up the "tailings pond" as was recounted in a Cobbwebs column last year. When needed, we put in some time on the "Grizzly" which was a grate of railroad rails upon which dump trucks deposited loads of ore scraped from a huge pit further up Mt. Davidson. The "Grizzly" man had to take a big sledge hammer and break rocks so they'd pass through the grate into the rock crusher.

More often, our chores included stoking the ovens. These were big semi-circle pans under which firewood was kept burning. The troughs were regularly filled with mud. That is, the most valuable deposits from the mill's process, called "concentrates" were taken in half-liquid form, in a huge tub-like wheelbarrow.

This gooey load was poured into the heated pans or ovens. It was no mean feat to trundle the heavy barrow across the steaming, slippery and very hot ovens. (The soles of our shoes burned through in a couple of weeks.) We blithely pushed the sloppy loads with no fear—until a fellow worker fell into one of the heat pans and severely scalded his legs.

The liquid concentrate dried out in the heated ovens. Then the workmen had to shovel the dried lumps back into a small wheelbarrow. This was pushed up an incline to a small crusher which we labeled "the coffee grinder." This broke up the lumps, and reduced the dried concentrates to dust. Great clouds of powdery dust swirled up into the pouring gentleman's face. But most of it poured down a chute into another barrow.

Next step was to trundle the load of this highly valuable gold powder across the room to be shoveled into large sacks. Regularly, trucks came to the mill to haul these sacks of goodies to the smelter in California.

We worked the "graveyard shift" which was from 11 p.m. to 7 a.m. One morning, about 6:30, we pushed a laden wheelbarrow across the room, but met disaster. The wheel hit a knothole, or something, and overturned!

The fine, powdery gold dust flowed all over the floor! It seemed to be everywhere as the small clouds settled.

"My God, it's all over!" exclaimed a fellow workman.

"I bet there was a thousand dollars worth in that load," gasped another.

Daunted but desperate, we all seized brooms and swept. And swept, and swept. No one knows how much, if any, of the dust-like concentrates sifted through cracks in the floor. But we got almost all of it swept up and shoveled into the bag—just as the superintendent of the mill, Mr. Arch McFarland, drove up to begin his day.

"What's doing, boys?" he asked pleasantly.

"Oh, we're just sweeping up, Mr. McFarland," we all responded.

Pleased, he stated, "That's fine, boys, keep the place neat and clean."

"Yes, sir, Mr. McFarland," we chorused, "Yes, sir!"

—August 15, 1982

He was to keep his identity and mission secret until the time he was to be summoned back to headquarters to report

Recently Edwin Meese, counselor to the President of the United States, gave the traditional Jackson Address before the National Judicial College in Reno. The occasion was the "graduation" of more than 100 judges who had completed their refresher courses at the prestigious college at University of Nevada. Among the magistrates who took the latest course to bring themselves up-to-date in jurisprudence were judges from more than 30 states, as well as from the Air Force, Army, Shoshone Indian Tribe (Nevada), and the countries of Japan and Thailand.

Meese prefaced his address with a story about the Central Intelligence Agency, asserting that CIA officials had groomed one agent for a secret mission. Briefing the agent, they told him he was to be a covert observer in a foreign country—keeping his identity and mission secret until the time he was to be summoned back to headquarters to report.

He was given the new name of Murphy, and was assigned to live in a small village in Ireland, under strict orders not to let anyone know his real business, and not to communicate with CIA headquarters in Washington. At the proper time, he was instructed, another agent would be sent to seek him out. The password by which he would know the agent would be the remark: "It's a beautiful day today, but tomorrow will be lovelier."

Months, and then years went by and finally the CIA bigwigs thought they'd better bring secret agent "Murphy" back to Washington. Another CIA expert was sent to seek him out, always in the covert manner, and by using the password only.

The new man found his way to the village in Ireland and looked around. Visiting the local pub, he remarked to the bartender he was looking for a man named Murphy.

"Well," said the barkeep, "We've several Murphys here. If you want Murphy the farmer, he lives one mile down that lane, if it's Murphy the shoemaker, his shop is at the end of this block. As a matter of fact, my name is Murphy, too."

Glancing around stealthily, the CIA agent remarked: "It's a beautiful day today, but tomorrow will be lovelier!"

"Oh," responded the bartender, "it must be Murphy the Spy you're looking for!" —*November 7, 1982*

Hanging up his stars or learning early to go to the top

An angry, lonesome boy left his stepfather's Nevada ranch house, mounted his horse and rode 15 miles to Lovelock. From then on he was alone—living by himself in a tiny shack, determined to get an education no matter how many obstacles a 13-year-old would face. That determination carried him through high school, college and a half-century in the Army. He became one of the most respected officers in the military/educational field.

This week Eugene Salet hung up his stars, or put them in a frame or drawer, or whatever a retiring general does with his insignia.

Gene Salet (pronounced "Salay") was born in tiny Standish, Lassen County, Calif., before the family moved to a Pershing County ranch. After his parents died, Salet lived with his stepfather, but it became intolerable. He decided to go it alone and rode his horse to Lovelock. He found a small shack to live in, which cost $10 a month to rent. He paid for rent and food by milking cows for neighbors, and later by delivering milk and ice to the Lovelock people.

Summers, he worked at better-paying jobs. While in high school, he hopped a freight train to the Black Rock Desert, where he got a job as an "extra" in a Ronald Coleman movie. Another summer, he ran an electric car hauling ore out of a Pershing mine. When burdens became

Two famous heavyweight champions, Max Baer and Jack Dempsey—I know them both well. The little guy is Ancil Hoffman, Baer's manager.

too heavy, he'd hop a freight train, and "ride to anywhere" (and back to Lovelock).

General Salet credits football as the motivating force in keeping him going. He played all sports at Pershing High, but football was his best one. The University of Nevada lacked a widespread football recruiting program then, but the coaches gave him a scholarship.

"I had just 50 cents in my pocket when I arrived in Reno," he recalls. He had made the trip from Lovelock via freight train. He went directly to the president's office, and borrowed $500—no mean feat then or now. "I learned early to go to the top."

Salet also joined the Sigma Alpha Epsilon fraternity and got the job as head dishwasher. He soon had the fraternity pledges scrubbing the plates, pots and pans.

The wiry athlete, with his sleek black hair and lean good looks, was popular on campus. He graduated in 1934 with a commission from the ROTC Army Reserve. He then taught at Dayton High and other schools, frequently visiting Virginia City to sing. (He also refereed basketball games and I recall one where he growled at me to shut up or he'd kick me out of the game.)

He requested active duty in the Army in 1941, when it became obvious World War II was about to descend on the U.S. From then on, it was action and more action for the second lieutenant. He was a company battalion leader of a machine gun group, and fought on the front line for nearly two years in North Africa, Sicily, Italy and France.

By 1944, the soldier had risen to rank of lieutenant colonel. It would take a whole column to list all the wartime decorations won by Gene Salet—Silver Star and Bronze Star with clusters, Legion of Merit, the Croix de Guerre from France, Military Valor Cross from Italy and many more.

After World War II, Salet was appointed to numerous stations within the Army, including government work on Okinawa. And in the South Pacific, he worked in atomic bomb testing, which, he confesses, has caused him deep anxiety about nuclear warfare.

After retiring from active duty, Salet became dean at the prestigious Georgia Military College. He later became president of the college and was elected national president of the U.S. Association of Military Colleges. Meanwhile, he took an active role in civilian life and was honored for his civic activity, receiving honorary degrees from Dickinson University and a university in Okinawa. He prizes the "Distinguished Nevadan" award granted by his alma mater in Reno.

Honored at a full military review recently, General Salet's retirement speech stressed these ideals: "Duty, honor, country, character."

—*July 3, 1985*

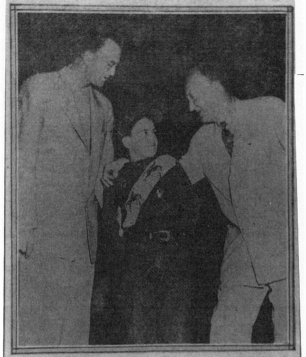

Three Cobbs--and All Named Ty

TY COBB NIGHT at Moana Park, home of the Reno Far West League club, spotlighted two other Ty Cobbs in addition to the famed Georgia Peach. Left to right, Ty Cobb, sports editor of the Nevada State Journal, Reno; his 10-year-old son, Ty, and the Detroit Tiger immortal. Both Sports Editor Cobb and his son are namesakes of the former American League star, who is a resident of Lake Tahoe, Nevada. The Georgia Peach was presented with a scroll and a golf caddy cart at the ceremonies.

Three Ty Cobbs. It was Ty Cobb Night at Moana ball park, and I was the M.C. The honoree was the immortal Ty Cobb of baseball fame. The boy is my son Ty Jr., later an Army colonel, advisor to President Reagan, and now head of the Yosemite National Institutes.

The capper was the delivery of divorce papers, which was quite a surprise to my wife

It was bad enough to pack the same name through youth, I took quite a razzing, especially playing sandlot baseball and softball.

It got downright confusing when the baseball great moved to Nevada. In the early 1950s, he bought a lakeshore lodge near Cave Rock, Lake Tahoe, and spent most of his later years there. He opened an account at the same Reno bank at which my more meager savings were deposited. His phone number wasn't listed, so I received many long-distance calls from all over. One of the most persistent was developer-baseball owner Del Webb.

I got telegrams and mail from persons who knew that baseball's Ty Cobb lived somewhere in Nevada. I got his bills, including his tax bills from the State of California. The Great One had a habit of advertising for lost articles, including a prized fountain pen, and giving my Reno address as the place to bring the items and get a reward. One time a person came leading two yelping dogs which Tyrus Raymond had lost.

The capper was the delivery of his divorce papers, which was quite a surprise to my wife.

But Cobb didn't impose on my family and me. He frequently visited our Reno home and had us over for southern meals. Once he offered to finance my son in a Lake Tahoe chemical garbage can business, and was hurt when the lad turned it down for a ranch summer job.

The older Cobb cherished a "Ty Cobb Night" given by the Reno Silver Sox at Moana Stadium, where a photo was taken of us with my son, Ty, who was about 11 then. The photo of the three T.C.s was published by the *Sporting News* of St. Louis in its annual yearbook.

One of the elder Cobb's favorite stories was about the time he attended an Eagles Lodge affair in Carson City, and was approached by a man who said: "Mr. Cobb, at last I have a chance to tell you that I always admired…"

"Well, thank you, sir," responded the celebrity who had heard the compliment hundreds of times. "… your column in the Nevada State

Journal," continued the other person.

The confusion in names became well known. Several years ago a feature about it appeared in *Editor and Publisher,* the newspaper trade magazine.

In spite of the difference in ages and eras, I guess the confusion is natural. Tyrus Raymond Cobb is continually labeled "immortal" and people regard him as a timeless legend.

Once, when I was playing in a softball game in Sparks, a small lad approached me for an autograph.

"Sorry, son, you've got the wrong person," I said.

"Oh, no," he insisted; "I know who you are. You're one of the IMMORALS of baseball!" —*September 7, 1985*

Polishing up a tarnished sport

I never lost a knockout. (Never scored one, either.) I never lost a decision. (Never won one, either.)

With this explanation of my non-existent boxing career, you might wonder why I have been selected for the World Boxing Hall of Fame.

Me too. But the hall, based in Los Angeles, figures that contributions to the sport by non-participants also justify selection. Without due modesty, we recall these efforts on behalf of boxing:

I covered, at ringside, hundreds of Golden Gloves, AAU, collegiate and professional bouts, giving at least one paragraph to even the most obscure combatants.

Established a new division in the Golden Gloves—when amateur boxing peaked in Nevada, a special high school novice division.

Served on the committee which conducted the National Collegiate Athletic Association championship tournament in Reno in 1959.

Directed the Nevada-Eastern California trials for the Olympic Games, and managed the team of champions to the Western Regionals in San Francisco.

But we think what convinced officials of the hall of fame—which will conduct induction ceremonies Nov. 1 at L.A.'s Airport Marriott

Hotel—to pick a rural ex-sports writer was this title: "Father of the Nevada Boxing Commission."

Again, throwing modesty to the wind, we're grateful this contribution has been remembered and recognized.

In the late 1930s, in my first years as a *Nevada State Journal* sportswriter, ring activity flourished here—but not all of it was commendable.

There were abuses on all sides. Poorly-conditioned "boxers" appeared on cards. Some who fought in Reno had been KO'd a few days before in California. There was seldom a doctor in attendance. There were no pre-fight medical exams. And there were frequent no-shows of advertised main eventers. Run-outs were occasional and non-punishable.

Catalyst for reform was a kind of run-out by a world contender. Lou Nova, a high-ranked contender who lost to Joe Louis in a title bout, was training in Carson City following an illness. His opponent on a Labor Day card in Reno was to be Tom Jordan, a prison guard who had recently sparred with Nova.

Virtually no one bought tickets in advance, and on the day of the bout Nova's manager refused to let his fighter go through with the show. The card was canceled and promoter Johnny Gammick took a financial bath. There was no commission to appeal to or to enforce any agreement. Furious, Gammick, now deceased, went to work gathering information on state boxing boards around the country.

Since I had campaigned frequently in my *Journal* column for such an authority, I sifted through many documents and letters, picked out the best points, and submitted the proposal to one man who could carry it on—my father.

Storey County Sen. Will Cobb had the legislative bill-drafter formulate a bill, which he then introduced in the Nevada Legislature—and it was passed.

On April 9, 1941, Nevada governor E.P. Carville signed the bill. It created a state athletic commission to govern ring sports, and was headed by William Lewis, warden of the Nevada Prison, and Wayne Hinckley, Reno fuel dealer. It also included M.C. Tinch of Las Vegas, A. Kellison of Sparks and Walter Collins of Ely.

Over the years, the appointive board has had ups and downs. But, generally, it has been dedicated to running the sport cleanly, accurately and with compassion. It has inaugurated licensing of athletes, with agreements of other states to cooperate in suspensions.

It has required good medical examinations, training and supervision of judges and referees, medical presence at the bouts and financial security from promoters.

In the past two decades, the Nevada Athletic Commission has supervised more world title bouts than any other state commission in the U.S. As far as we can recall, there has been only one tragedy to mar a long era of success. —*October 29, 1986*

They were rowed in a boat across the river to aplace where they were sheltered in an outhouse, and by light of a lantern, their bloody wounds were sewn up

Piper's Opera House, the large wooden structure at B and Union streets in the famous mining camp of Virginia City, is not very beautiful, but it is picturesque and holds the affection of Nevadans far and wide.

It was built in 1876, following the great fire of the preceding year that destroyed most of Virginia City. It was operated by John Piper, who was associated with theaters and entertainment in Reno as well as on the Comstock.

It once resounded to the rich voice of Enrico Caruso, and saw performances by Ada Mencken, Lillie Langtry, David Belasco and many more. And the story reminded me of a man who was closely associated with Piper's, Dan Connors, who was one of the most interesting characters I ever knew.

He lived right behind the Opera House, on A Street, and the Cobbs lived next door to the Connors' house for 40 years. It is now better known as the Lucius Beebe house, after the late flamboyant author, editor and gourmet who acquired the two-story mansion and restored it with 19th-century decor.

But in my youth, it was the Dan Connors house.

Dan Connors, Sr. had a colorful career—including being a bare-knuckled prizefighter, manager of a world lightweight champion (Frank Erne), boxing instructor, a ring reporter for New York newspapers, manager of a vaudeville troupe and manager of Piper's Opera House, where he brought the first movies to Nevada.

He was raised in the East, where his skillful fists first won him acclaim as a fighter, although fisticuffs were illegal in most states then.

He told me of one battle on the outskirts of Philadelphia that was raided by the police. The two opponents and some friends escaped the raiders, and were rowed in a boat across the river to a place where they were sheltered in an outhouse, and by light of a lantern, their bloody wounds were sewn up.

Connors bore the marks of his first profession—layers of scar tissue around his battered eyebrows, rows of broken bones protruding from his hands and a battered ear known in the trade as "cauliflower ear."

Dan progressed to the role of instructor, and in the 1890s he operated a boxing school in a New York City gymnasium. Thus he acquired the title of "professor."

He was engaged by various New York newspapers to cover the big fights of the era, including those of John L. Sullivan. Professor Connors first visited Nevada in 1897, when he came out to cover the Jim Corbett-Bob Fitzsimmons fight in Carson City. That was apparently for the *New York Sun.*

He came back in 1910 for the Jim Jeffries-Jack Johnson fight in Reno, according to his son Ed, who is now retired in Carson. (Another son, Dan, Jr., is also retired and living in Reno.)

Professor Connors liked Nevada and stayed here. He married Lavina Berry, who was the widow of one of the Piper family.

(There were a lot of Piper relatives then, and even now. Among them is Mrs. Louise Zimmer Driggs, who spent large sums of money in recent years restoring the picturesque but decaying theater building. She also restored the small house on Union Street, adjacent to the Opera House, which was owned by the Piper clan. The last residents there that I remember were Hazel Piper, a blind woman of musical talent, and her sister, Lou Devaney.)

Dan Connors had performed in vaudeville, and managed a traveling company of entertainers. And his brother ran a concession at New York's Coney Island. Through these connections, Dan obtained one of the newfangled motion-picture machines and brought to Virginia City the first movies, a subject we will detail in the next column.

—*July 1, 1987*

The crowd vented anger by throwing objects at the screen and threatening to mob the projectionist

This is the second of three columns on Piper's Opera House in Virginia City.

When we last left Dan Connors, he had performed in vaudeville and managed a traveling company of entertainers. His brother ran a concession at New York's Coney Island, and through these connections Dan obtained a newfangled motion-picture machine and brought the first movies to Virginia City.

That was before the days of sound, of course, and Dan projected the silents on a big screen in Piper's Opera House. (I recall seeing the jerky movements of the actors, punctuated by streaks and dots on the screen; and we kids set up great clamor whenever a breakdown interrupted the picture.)

The movies were silent, yes, but Connors provided appropriate sound to go with the film. His son, Eddie, recalls he had some homemade sound-effects devices:

"He had a kind of machine, wood and canvas, with openings. And when you turned a crank fast, it sounded like a heavy wind. This was used to add realism to movies of windstorms, typhoons, etc."

Dan also had a contraption, behind the screen, a collection of pieces of tin, iron and glass. At the appropriate time, two boys would tip over the box and pour out all the stuff, thus creating a tremendous crash. This accompanied train wrecks and other catastrophes of the screen—so vividly and loudly that people in the audience screamed in alarm.

Ed Connors remembers more realism from the chickens.

"There was a comedy involving chickens, like some thieves raiding a chicken coop. Dad had several chickens behind the movie screen and at the right time, the kids would disturb them so they'd start clucking loudly. It sounded real."

There was no theater marquee to advise citizens of the films to be shown. But I recall there was a large round board containing many light globes, hung just above one of the front doors, and when we'd see that all lit up, we rejoiced to know there was a movie coming up.

During Dan Connors' heyday, Piper's Opera House had many uses. It served as a meeting hall for the citizens of Virginia City. There were also boxing cards, basketball games and skating.

But in the days of pioneering movies in Nevada, Connors branched out, taking his projector, screen and rolls of film to nearby towns like Dayton. The latter was a disastrous venture, however.

Dayton was largely populated by Italians, mainly first-generation people who still had close ties to their homeland.

One of the comedy films which Connors took to Dayton was intended to amuse the audience, since the can of film was labeled "Italian comedy." However, the citizens were not amused, particularly by a scene which purported to show the "King of Italy" eating spaghetti made of rubber.

The slapstick antics with the bouncy, snappy spaghetti irked the spectators. So did other scenes, and the crowd vented anger by throwing objects at the screen and threatening to mob the projectionist.

Connors later stated he was saved from violence by the intervention of husky Americo Giani, the town blacksmith. At that, Connors barely got to his horse and buggy and hastened out of town before he got roughed up.

Connors' wife died around 1918, and he was left to raise two small boys. At the end of the 1920s he gave up active management of Piper's Opera House.

With that, the activity shifted to National Guard Hall, a huge stone structure on the main street, where further dances and basketball games were held. The movies were seen there at Cole's Theater, in the same building.

But fearing a possible fire in the venerable Piper's, Dan Connors padlocked the building where Lola Montez and Maude Adams once strutted on the sloping stage, where the great Caruso sang, and where Ada Mencken rode her horse to "eternity." —*July 8, 1987*

Of trap doors and rites of passage

Having given up management of Piper's Opera House, Virginia City's Dan Connors, an aging ex-fighter and producer, became a recluse, seldom venturing from his kitchen in the rear of the "Black Mansion." However, he always welcomed my visits (I was still a teenager), and shared with me vivid recollections of the big fights of the 1890s. With a few exceptions, Connors resented visitors and refused to allow them into the padlocked opera house across the street.

One exception was Max Baer. The big fellow who once held the world's heavyweight title visited Connors a couple of times. Once, he spent two hours conversing with the one-time bare-knuckle pugilist, and later he sent Connors a photo inscribed: "To Dan Connors, who fought before they wore pillows on their hands."

To some unwelcome visitors, he would turn his head and point to his gnarled and puffed ear, saying: "Now tell it to the cauliflower."

As mentioned before, we lived next door. One day, hearing a commotion, my mother exclaimed, "You better go over to Connors' house; I think he's in trouble."

The trouble belonged not to Connors but to two pushy characters from Hollywood. They wanted to get into Piper's Opera House and became obnoxious when denied entry. It developed into a shoving affair—which then erupted. When I got there, one fellow was on the bottom step, holding his bleeding nose, and the other was draped halfway over the railing, dazed.

Into his late years, the old gentleman kept in condition with exercise and long, solitary walks. He exercised with Indian clubs, which were long wooden objects shaped like bowling pins. He would whirl these around his head and chest in intricate routines, until one day he accidentally bashed himself in the mouth.

With my daughter Patricia.

Although the opera house was kept padlocked in the 1940s, I often joined the teenage Connors boys by going in through our secret passage. We entered through a hole burrowed under a wooden sidewalk on the side of the great, silent arena. We found great boxes filled with roller skates and spent hours whizzing around the dark hall.

This was the same entrance through which I once escorted one of America's favorite and most famous actor-humorist, Will Rogers. Accompanied by another old-time actor, Fred Stone, Rogers was prowling around outside the famous old opera house when he saw me. He coaxed me to help him make an entry, and I guided him and Stone through our secret passage.

They were delighted, despite the conditions. Later, covered with spider webs and dust, the great humorist emerged into daylight. He was clutching something he had found beneath the old stage, a poster depicting some entertainment of the 1800s.

The actors' wives were not pleased by the grubby appearance of their spouses. However, I took Rogers and Stone up to visit Connors, who received them graciously. Later, Rogers was quoted as saying, "Dan Connors was born 50 years too soon," as he recounted the clever devices used by the pioneering theater magnate to augment his early-day silent films.

Connors, "The Professor of Boxing," died in 1945, while his sons were away during World War II.

Three decades later, the vacant building was acquired by Louise Driggs, who renovated it. She had a new foundation put in below the sagging walls and restored much of the interior. At various times, Piper's Opera House has been open to visitors, via a caretaker. And, occasionally, programs of classical music have been staged there.

Let's hope that if a sale is consummated, whoever the new owners may be will continue to make the historic 110-year-old structure available to a doting public. And that Professor Dan Connors, one of the most unforgettable characters we've ever known, would be pleased.

—July 15, 1987

When the Basques' money ran out, they headed back to the sheep ranges

Downtown Reno looks bright in several locations, but barren and grim in others. We're speaking of places which were once the sites of popular buildings and now are bare parking lots, the structures long-ago demolished. In particular, the block on Lake Street, east side, between Commercial Row and Second Street which, except for the surviving Mizpah Hotel, is a vast concrete plain.

We've already commented on the demolition of the popular hotel-bar-restaurant buildings, the Columbo and Toscano.

In reference to the Toscano, the well-patronized hangout of out-of-town Basques as well as Renoites, I recall the position of Joe Elcano, Sr. We've previously written about the great food and economical prices in the cafe which flourished for several decades. Paul Elcano, Sr. of Reno, son of the late Toscano owner, recalls his father's role as a sort of shepherd for the sheepherders.

The immigrants from the Pyrenees Mountains of Spain and France came over to work herding sheep on Nevada's hills and plains. They endured the eternal baas of the ewes, rams and lambs; maintained their flocks in rugged terrain and miserable weather, and survived the loneliness.

But after a year, each sheepherder was going to town. That meant Reno. And the livestock owners agreed that the weather-beaten herders needed a vacation. They would head for Reno and go to the Toscano. Gave their pay checks to Joe Elcano. He cashed them all, put the money in labeled envelopes with each man's name and accounting written down. Elcano doled out the money to his guests as they desired—for shopping or a good time.

He kept current totals, and notified the Basques when their money was running out. Then they headed back to the sheep ranges.

Sometimes the livestock ranchers, in need of help, would come to Reno and visit the Toscano. With the help of host Elcano, they recruited new crews for the next season.

Paul Elcano says that the visiting herders who stayed at the Toscano hotel got room (upstairs over the bar-cafe), breakfast, a hearty Basque lunch, also dinner—for a total price of $1! —*February 22, 1989*

Diamond Lil was the first woman dealer in Nevada

A bit of Nevada gambling history passed on recently with the death of "Diamond Lil."

She died in San Francisco and her real name was Bernita Brooks, but few in Reno will remember that. She was known as Diamond Lil, which was dubbed by Raymond I. "Pappy" Smith.

Diamond Lil was probably the first woman dealer in Nevada, and thereby might have been the first in the nation.

Diamond Lil, tall and good-looking, attracted attention in a pastime known previously as an all-male profession. She was the dealer at the craps game at Harolds Club, and Pappy Smith was proud of her, calling the attention of his guests and visitors to the lady handling the dice.

It was not long after she broke the barrier that women dealers became the vogue in the state where casino gambling was first legalized.
—April 19, 1989

The lawyer calmly, with arms crossed on his chest, faced the gun-totin' bully

Recently, we had a column item about a friend who came across a 1905 magazine which featured prominent figures at fashionable Newport, R.I. It included stocky, white-bearded William Stewart, U.S. Senator from Nevada. This item has stirred some curiosity, and we have a little background on William Stewart.

In the early days of Nevada, when it was a territory, "bad men" were the gun-slinging bullies who terrorized the bars and mines of this part of these parts.

One was Sam Brown, who was reputed to have killed a large number. Hearing that one of his cronies was on trial in Genoa, Brown made a dramatic entrance. According to Robert Laxalt's book of Nevada history, it was like a scene from a movie melodrama. As Brown burst into the courtroom, the spectators and attendants scattered, most diving out the windows. The room was virtually empty when the much-feared bad man advanced toward the young prosecuting attorney—William Stewart. The lawyer calmly, with arms crossed on his chest, faced the gun-totin' bully. He uncrossed his arms, revealing a Derringer pistol in each hand! He marched the desperado to the witness stand and forced him to give testimony about his partner in crime.

Enraged at his public humiliation, the gun-slinger Brown rode away. As he passed a Carson Valley ranch and small inn owned by Henry Van Sickle, Brown took a shot at the latter. Van Sickle, who had been harassed in the past by the bully, loaded his shotgun and took off in pursuit. Brown stayed just ahead of his pursuer, who fired several blasts at him, but missed. As darkness came on, Van Sickle took a short cut. Some stories indicate it was at lower Gold Hill, south of Virginia City. He got ahead of Brown and met the desperado on the road. One blast from the shotgun blew off his head, ending the vicious career of the notorious "chief."

The coroner's jury not only exonerated Van Sickle, but praised him, and urged that he be made sheriff. —*June 21, 1989*

She campaigned against booze
and smashed up saloons with her hatchet

Scarcely any columns we have written in 24 years aroused such interest as the two recently on Commercial Row.

The fact that the city government of Reno is apparently consenting to abandon at least part of the old-time street to enhance expansion of a big casino-hotel seems to be most timely.

People maintaining business in the Commercial Row area have protested such a move, but the city administration appears willing to go along with anything the casinos and developers desire.

Old Commercial Row was created over 120 years ago as Reno's main business street. For at least a century, many businesses flourished on Commercial Row's four or five blocks paralleling the railroad tracks.

Although Commercial is now mainly a back door to several big gambling casinos, there were many decades of stores, saloons and cafes. And the number of phone calls and letters to this writer showed the interest in this one-time bustling street in downtown Reno.

A lot of comments concerned Cannan's Drug Store. Due to an unfortunate typo, it came out "Vannan's" (with a V) in the first column. Clyde Cannan operated it as a drug store for years, and included a section of medical items for livestock. Owners of horses, cattle and sheep patronized this section. Clyde also had a floral shop in the alley.

Eddie Hill, retired Washoe public administrator, recalled that as a boy in 1930 he was the delivery boy for Cannan's. Pete Walters recalled the Reno Meat Market as an old-fashioned shop with sawdust

> **SHACKLED**
>
> *Two Reno women, preparing to depart for a sorority reunion or some- such, were being feted by friends Sunday evening. As a joke, some- one brought out an old pair of leg- irons and clamped one of the re- strainers around the still fairly-well- turned ankle of one of the girls. It was good for a laugh—but the real hilarity came when it was discov- ered that the key wouldn't open the lock. Police and sheriff's officeres took turns at trying keys, but to no avail. When last seen, the lady, carrying the loose end of the shackle device, was heading for a machine shop or someplace where there was a good hacksaw.—June 19, 1967*

on the floor and huge chopping blocks behind the counter. Also the barrel of sauerkraut near the door.

Harold Curran was interested in the item about the original surveyor's stake from which the townsite was laid out by the Central Pacific surveyors in 1868. He said his family later lived at that site, and a big cottonwood tree grew right at the place where the first stake was placed.

Craig Questa notes that his great-grandfather, G.B. Questa, operated a "dry-goods" store on Commercial Row, next to Reno Meat. He took over that site in 1912, formerly occupied by Zenda Store, which in turn was a brewery back in the 1890s.

Lou Spitz says he fondly remembers Jackass Johnny's, where you could get a 10-cent beer and a "free lunch" which consisted of cheese, crackers and bologna. Well-appreciated by college students during the Great Depression.

Chuck Dromiak recalled that his great-uncle Alex built and operated the biggest hotel on Commercial Row (and Center Street) for years. Dromiak noted that his ancestor, Alex, was a leader in shutting Reno's door to the famous temperance crusader, Carrie Nation. She was the one who campaigned against booze, even smashing up saloons with her hatchet, and making fiery speeches. She was scheduled to make such a speech in Reno, says Chuck Dromiak. But Alex rounded up indignant bar owners from all over the city. A large and irate number of anti-temperance people gathered at the railroad depot. When Carrie Nation tried to descend from her train, the solid gathering of the pro-whiskey crowd actually prevented her from leaving the train steps, let alone make a speech in Reno. —*October 18, 1989*

Depression teens

"How was it, being a teenager growing up during the Great Depression?" That was the question popped to me by a Reno taxicab driver, a young black man who said he, too, had problems being a youngster in a depressed area. But he had read a lot about the Great Depression and was curious as to the conditions. I felt well qualified to answer that one, having become a teenager when the worst financial blight hit the U.S. public. The Depression began right after the stock market crash of 1929. The immediate effects were slower in hitting Nevada, but they seemed to last longer. The worst period, for me, was my high-school era from 1930 to 1933. To sum it up we didn't have a lot of things, but we didn't complain very much because we didn't know any better. We had:

No school bus
No school cafeteria
No shop (woodworking manual training, craft)
No home economics classes
No, or infrequent, movies
No school baseball, or football, or track , or basketball teams
No television, of course
No recreation rooms or clubs
No school student newspaper
No school yearbook
No cars
No school band (nor any music classes)
No drugs
No ski slopes, chair lifts, rope tows

Times were tough all over. There was a limited amount of activity in the dying mines. There were very few jobs, especially for teen-agers. The county paid meager pensions to widows and elderly people. These were published in the weekly newspaper, and I wondered how these unfortunates even existed on those little checks. Three grocery stores carried many people on credit. I doubt if many of those bills were ever paid. The grocery stores did provide part-time work for young fellows, driving the delivery trucks or the horse-drawn wagons. Several saloons remained open despite the tough times. The only "soda fountain" for young people was Billy Marks' Crystal Bar. For recreation, some of us boys played pool or billiards on the only tables, in the Smokery Saloon (now the Delta). When someone complained to owner Joe Viani about minors using pool tables in a place that also served adults liquor and had gambling (card) tables, Joe shrugged and asked: "Where else can they go?"

About those cars. The only one I remember was owned by the basketball team captain, who helped support himself and his widowed mother by delivering newspapers in the car. Sometimes a student would procure the family car. The kids piled in, two deep per seat, and "cruised Main." We drove to lower Gold Hill to partway out the Geiger Grade. Big stuff.

The rest of the time, in the evenings, we just walked in twos, threes, or larger groups. Simply walked the main street (C Street) from one end to the other, just walking and talking. For some of us there was access to the National Guard Hall where we boxed. In a small lobby illuminated by one light globe, we banged at each other heartedly. No one did any banking, because the banks were closed throughout the state. A lady who grew up in a small town at that time just remarked that people in those rural towns took care of each other. As far as we know, no one starved. People often went to the homes of ailing, elderly or jobless folks and did their chores, bought food, ran their errands. Our clothing was not ragged nor was it spiffy. The same corduroy pants, sweaters or skirts were worn day after day. It looks like I've run out of space for this account of being a teenager in the Great Depression. More next week.—*May 16, 1990*

We salvaged equipment for track and got shot puts from the rock-crusher ball mill of the Arizona-Comstock

Last week, the Neighbors section ran a Cobbwebs column with a different topic: "Being a Teenager During the Great Depression." I listed many things which teenagers of the time didn't enjoy; but we didn't complain because we didn't know any better.

In our high school, in the top floor of the ancient (1876) Fourth Ward School, our school board did its best to provide a basic education. The three teachers, usually fresh out of the University of Nevada, were paid meager salaries. They doubled up in duties. The high school principal also governed the middle school and grammar schools and doubled as a teacher. His office was also the administrative quarters and the school library. One male teacher doubled as sports coach. The woman teacher not only taught language and typing, but produced the infrequent school plays and coached the girl's basketball team.

Despite these efforts, we missed out on some things which were canceled because of the hard times. As an economy move, the school board had dropped "shop." No instruction any more in manual training (wood working) for the boys. They hung out in the room, which was also the janitor's quarters, and smoked cigarettes.

There was no playground. We teenagers did play softball at recess or before classes.

After one season, team football was abandoned by the school authorities. You can't hold down an active teen, however. We "borrowed" the stored-away football suits from an unlocked room and formed our own sandlot football team. We coached ourselves and wrote to Pop Warner of Stanford University; the old gent obliged by sending us some basic plays. We played on the quartz-strewn "Pan Mill" field, just off Six-Mile Canyon, and played similar youths from Gardnerville, Carson, Dayton, Reno and Sparks.

On the same field, once the site of the John Mackay-James Fair mill, we also played self-coached baseball. We also salvaged equipment for track and got shot puts from the rock-crusher ball mill of the Arizona-Comstock building.

As mentioned before, boxing was a popular activity. A few of our pugs did well in the Reno Golden Gloves; Norman Harris and Martin Rosso won titles. There were occasional dances, in the National Guard Hall, or in Dayton where big Gino Gianni got out his accordion after basketball games and provided the music.

Piper's Opera House was boarded up, but occasionally a movie effort was started in other locales. Sometimes we got up an expedition to Reno and took in the shows at the Majestic and Granada theaters. If we could muster up the 25-cent admission.

Part-time jobs were scarce. I had one starting up the stoves in the National Guard Hall to warm the big room for basketball practice, and I also started the stoves in the girls' and boys' dressing rooms.

One of the seasonal part-time jobs was ice cutting. When word spread "they're cutting ice" we all headed for the Divide Reservoir,

The last great gathering of world champion boxers was held in Reno in 1970. All world champs except Two-Ton Tony Galento, who almost was one. From left: Willie Pastrano, Fred Apostoli, Tony Galento, Jersey Joe Walcott, James Braddock, Jack Sharkey, Jackie Fields, Jimmy McLarrin. Photo at the Mapes Hotel.

which usually froze to a depth of two or more feet. It was bitter cold in that wind, as we manned the long-toothed saws and cut out blocks of ice. These were dragged out with hooks and transported to a building (the Ice House) for storage until summer. Masses of sawdust kept them from melting. There were always more willing workers than there were ice-cutting jobs.

During summers, we "rustled" for work in the few remaining mines. We usually hitchhiked down to Silver City and walked back up Gold Canyon (Gold Hill) from mine to mine, hoping to get a few days' work. Well, it looks like I've rambled through the allotted space. We'll finish this series next week. —*May 23, 1990*

I had the job of splitting these
chunks of pine with a sledgehammer

It's about time to wind up my long-winded recollection of "How It Was Being a Teenager in the Great Depression."

I mentioned the coveted part-time jobs. One was unloading the V&T cars. The chief fuel dealer was Louis Roth, who paid the boys for unloading the blocks of firewood or bags of coal onto his truck. These loads were transported to his "wood yard."

Most of us boys were occupied after school in our own yards. My father spent his one day off each week hauling in old logs from the hills and sawing them up on a home-rigged saw attached to his truck. I had the job of splitting these chunks of pine with sledgehammer and iron wedges, then chopping them to size and carrying them to the woodshed and to the kitchen woodbox.

There were other teenage chores, especially when the water pipes froze. Each morning of the deep freeze, before school, my neighbor Eddie Connors and I would open the nearby fire hydrant, which seldom froze, and fill tubs, boilers, pails, pots, etc., for domestic use. It took two of us to carry the big tubs and boilers.

I previously mentioned we had no yearbook. This was partially correct. The last one, "The Hot Water Plug," came out in 1931 when I was a sophomore. However, in my senior year, we did have a high-school news column in the weekly Virginia City News. I wrote this for Vincent Nevin, the last of the hand-set printers and editors.

As mentioned before, there were no bank accounts. Aside from having no money, anyway, people couldn't deposit anything because all the state's banks were closed. When I was elected student body president, I called for a treasurer's report at the first meeting. Harold Hunter gave it: "I've got 4 dollars in an envelope in the office (the principal's office) and $3.50 home in my other pants."

We never had a school bus. Basketball trips out of town were in loaned private cars, and we were accustomed to putting on chains up Gold Hill or the Geiger Grade. Once we had to hire a Virginia & Truckee special—one locomotive and one car—to get to a game in Carson or Stewart.

I have mentioned the clothing of the Great Depression. Every boy had a goal—a sheepskin overcoat. This was made of something like canvas, with a sheepskin collar. When outgrown, this garment was passed on to smaller kids. Our ultimate goal was the black leather-looking "sheepskin" coat, usually reserved for seniors.

The school-sponsored dances were strange affairs. The groups staging the dances often negotiated with Tony Pecetti to come up on his motorcycle and play his accordion. Sometimes we'd get a big band from Reno, consisting of a drummer, pianist and saxophone players. They'd begin with toe-tickling numbers until someone had the nerve to get out on the dance floor.

This was a rather embarrassing situation, because the elder ladies of the community always sat in the balcony of the National Guard Hall and took close notice. It was also difficult for a would-be dancer to cross the dance floor and ask one of the girls for the first dance. This sometimes marked one as "going steady" or snubbing the other gals. We often solved this by asking the girls from Dayton or Carson first, thereby avoiding "favoritism" among the home girls.

When the band played on and on and no one would start the dancing, principal John Gilmartin would go out to our group waiting outside. The fee was a dollar, which was out of our reach. So he'd say, "All right, come on. You can come in free." That started the dance. After midnight, the exhausted musicians would pass the hat, collecting cash for yet another round.

That's the end of the Great Depression, teenage variety. I'll probably hear from a lot of folks in their 70s and 80s telling me what I overlooked. OK. —*May 30, 1990*

Horrified, Betty tried to pull the tasty turk from the lion's jaws

The earliest days of Reno television were recalled recently when the Reno Ad Club staged a luncheon honoring Betty Stoddard Muncie, a "pioneer" of TV/radio talk shows.

"Coffee With Betty" and "Be My Guest" were the titles of the original and highly popular Betty Stoddard shows. (We call her by her former name.)

When KOLO-TV Channel 8 first went on the air, the "studio" consisted of one room with one camera. In the corners and other parts of the room were the "sets." It was all live television then, no taped and edited commercials or shows. The camera simply swung from one "set" to another as time went on.

One day, as Betty prepared for an ad concerning a sale of turkeys, she prepared a table on which rested a large roasted turkey. With this, she would later give the sales pitch.

Meanwhile, a guest on another program was Johnny Michaels, who operated the Christmas Tree resort on the Mount Rose Highway. His feature was a tame and very large African lion. The King of Beasts was docile and well-behaved during most of the program. Suddenly, he spotted the turkey.

Enticed by the sight, or smell, of the big bird, the lion reached over the table and hauled down the would-be prop for the ad. Horrified, Betty tried to pull the tasty turk from the lion's jaws.

They tugged with it, until the lion took a swipe at his opponent with a huge paw. One claw inflicted a severe scratch on the person of Betty.

As this was being recounted at the Ad Club luncheon, a speaker said that Betty's ankle was scratched. "Ankle, hell!" came the voice of the honoree. Most everyone there knew that she had been wounded on a part of her midsection, near a delicate location. As we recall, hasty first aid was applied to the injured area, but it was still bleeding and Betty was forced to come on with her live commercial standing behind an automobile which was being hawked for an advertisement.

Not only did the courageous announcer suffer a scratch from the lion's claw, but she later revealed, "He bit me, too. Twice on the fanny."

But the show must go on, as they say in the business, and she bravely completed the on-camera commercial. —*November 6, 1991*

A hangout for unlikely customers

Dick Evans, once a world-class middleweight contender, operated the Eastside Inn on East Fourth Street in Reno. The original Eastside Bar was a colorful place, far from luxurious but highly popular with patrons from all walks of life. It was the hangout for some unlikely customers, such as judges, attorneys and Harold and Raymond A. Smith of Harolds Club.

Its plain walls were plastered with pasted-on clippings about Dick's former fights, pictures and even a full-length photo of him in fighting pose. He also had a great collection of boxing movies, one of the world's best collections, and Dick often exchanged films with another noted figure, the late Jimmy Jacobs. The latter was once national handball champion and one of the first managers of Mike Tyson.

The bar was later remodeled into a tasteful, decorated facility, destroying the charm of the raunchy former bar. Among the features of the former was a squirting telephone. Dick had a fake telephone behind the bar. When he pressed a hidden button, the phone rang. When he handed the instrument to an unsuspecting patron, and when the latter answered the "call," a stream of water would squirt out from the mouthpiece and into the victim's face.

I saw one woman so treated. She had come in with her face well made up with mascara, lipstick, rouge and so forth. She took the water shot squarely in the face, and all her makeup dribbled down her face. She was not pleased.

But the most unforgettable incident with the squirting phone came one summer afternoon. I was the only other person in the place, having responded to Dick's urgent plea to come down and see something, a clipping or letter or something.

Suddenly the quiet was shattered by a roar, as a big motorcycle drove up and parked in front. In came one of the most formidable bruisers I ever saw. He had a bushy beard, long pig-tailed hair, an earring, a leather vest and brawny bare arms covered with tattoos.

He swaggered in and roared: "Hey, have any of the cycle boys (he called it sickle) been in?"

Dick asked his name and responded, "Yeah, they were just here. They asked for you."

Then the secret telephone rang. Dick "answered" and told the tough guy: "It's for you."

The unsuspecting biker picked up the phone and—swoosh, he got a faceful of water.

"Oh, oh," I thought. "We're in for it now." But instead of the expected brawl, we were mystified when the husky cyclist, wiping his face with the bar towel, started to cry.

We asked why he was crying. Tearfully, he explained. "You guys are wonderful. No one in my life has ever paid any attention to me, and you think enough of me to pull a joke. I thank you. You make me happy."

With that, he went out, mounted his motorcycle and roared away. I breathed a sigh of relief, and Dick just grinned.

—November 18, 1992

Painting myself into a corner

This is the story of a date I almost had with a celebrity. Back in the late 1930s, when I was a young and single sportswriter for the *Nevada State Journal*, I was invited to a party.

It was to be a dinner party honoring the birthday of Zelda McKay. She was the daughter of Jim McKay, partner of Bill Graham, who operated the famous Bank Club gambling casino as well as the Cal-Neva Lodge at Lake Tahoe and other interests. Zelda was a very nice young lady, and I was honored to be invited to the party on the second floor of Club Fortune, predecessor of the present-day Cal Neva Club.

The people arranging the party said to me, "There's a young girl now singing at the lake. We would like you to be her escort for Zelda's birthday party."

I agreed, tentatively, and asked my boss at the newspaper if I could take that night off. "Hell, no," he exclaimed, "that's a basketball night, and we need you to handle it."

I had painted myself into a corner when I organized coverage of high school basketball all over Nevada and eastern California. Every hamlet which had a basketball team cooperated by phoning in the box scores and data on their home games. It took me and an array of "Journal Jocks"—weekend help—to take the calls, write the stories and get them out to the printers before deadline. The results were eagerly read in every town the next morning. It was a must to get the accounts in print.

Regretfully, I canceled my appearance at the McKay party. I don't know who wound up as the escort for the young singer. And that's the story of my "almost" date with Judy Garland.—*January 27, 1993*

The engine block was cracked

The other day, as I was paying the bill to the Department of Motor Vehicles for owning an automobile, I remembered it has been years since I first owned one. It was something like 59 or 60 years ago when I acquired a one-fourth share of ownership of an auto in Virginia City.

We had just come through a tremendous winter, when snow was piled three or four feet deep. Yes, it did snow back in those days.

Some fellow who roomed at a building on B Street across from Piper's Opera House, had left his car parked out on the street all winter. When the snow had melted, he tried to start it, in vain. The freezing weather took its toll, and the engine block was cracked. He simply gave the car to several of us teenagers, "Boys, take it. The car is yours."

It was a simple transaction and there were no paperwork documents, no legal bill of sale or such. Just "take it."

We conferred with my uncle, George Harris, who ran a garage on C Street, now the site of a big casino. He said he would try to weld the cracked block, if we brought it down. We disengaged the engine, and four of us placed the heavy engine on two crowbars and with each toting an end of a bar, lugged it down to the Harris garage.

We were starting down Union Street, near Piper's Opera House, when someone let his hold on the crowbar slip. The motor crashed to the ground and rolled down the short block to C Street. We retrieved it there and packed it the rest of the way to the garage. George Harris happened to be in front of his station and watched the action in amazement. "Boys, when I said to bring it down I didn't mean for you to roll it all the way!"

It was a difficult job, but he did weld up the crack in the engine block. Sufficient to allow operation of the engine when we got it re-engaged in the frame. It ran fairly well, except for the fact that somehow the fuel line from the gasoline tank to the engine had been broken by the freeze. We repaired this in a crude, if novel, way.

We got a large coffee can, fastened it to the engine with wires and ran a short hose or tube into the carburetor. This actually worked. The problem was the coffee can quickly ran empty. We carried a big can of gasoline and replenished the coffee can at short intervals. The car actually ran well, except for some overheating. Often when we turned off the ignition key, the engine kept rolling.

We soon tired of this novelty, and when notified that we had to buy a license for the car, we decided to get rid of it. We sold it for $15.

At the same time, we were warned that we should obtain drivers' licenses.

Unsure of the procedure, I walked down to the Storey County Courthouse. There Sheriff Dave Elkins, a kindly old gentleman, fished around in his desk and found an application form. As I was only 16 or 17, we were unsure of the age limits. But he filled out the form and gave me a little paper which qualified me for an official license. There was no written test required, nor any road test of driving skill.

I guess Mr. Elkins felt he should add something to this ceremony. Looking me in the eye, he asked: "You will be careful, won't you?"

"Yes, sir," I responded. And that was that. —*May 26, 1993*

The Dog House was Reno's
most-known and patronized honky-tonk

I have been thinking a lot about the Dog House. When I first went to work for the *Nevada State Journal* back in 1937, the newspaper was right next door to the Dog House, in the middle of the 100 block of North Center Street.

The Dog House was Reno's most-known and patronized honky-tonk. It was a combination dance hall entertainment center, gambling casino and restaurant. It featured round-the-clock entertainment, although this dwindled considerably in the early daylight hours.

Since closing, the site of the Dog House has been occupied by a bowling alley, night club, and Harrah's employment center.

The Dog House had a band, which played loudly at intervals, while an emcee introduced a variety of acts—tap dancers, vocalists, magicians, strippers, fan dancers and many more acts. The bandstand was on the south side of the place and since there was a thin wall between the club and the newspaper, often the music could be heard where we reporters hung out.

The Dog House room was encircled by rugged rustic tables, where patrons imbibed drinks of Chinese cuisine. My girlfriend at that time was the Chinese fan dancer, whose hours of appearance in the floor shows precluded much in the way of romance. She came out nude, but the customers got only tantalizing glimpses of her slender figure which she kept concealed by fast-moving feathery fans.

I could tell when her number was nearly over by the bump-and-grind music of the band drifting through the thin walls. Then I would go out our rear exit by a loading dock and to the next-door dock where the Chinese cooks were preparing their veggies. The dancer, having donned a bathrobe, would come out to meet me.

In the southeast corner was the lunch counter, presided over by Mr. T.F. Gee. I still remember his pork noodles. Gee and I were friends until his death a couple of years ago. A graduate of the University of California-Berkeley, he turned from engineering to cookery and later operated the Chinese Pagoda in Sparks, then on South Virginia Street, and later on West Fourth.

There was also a small gambling casino. —*July 7, 1993*

We hustled to procure a dime for admission

"The End of An Era…" That's what the last sign on the theater marquee stated … or something like that.

Yes, closing of the Granada Theater marked the last of the popular movie theaters in Reno. I'm not sure just when the Granada, on West First Street, was constructed and opened. But I do remember it was going strong in the late 1920s. The other theaters in Reno which flourished for many years were the Majestic, the Wigwam and the Tower.

We kids preferred the Majestic, a very large building at the corner of First and Center. The Saturday matinee was a date we youngsters waited all week for. We hustled to procure a dime for admission, as money was tight even then. Usually we sold bottles, as the milk company and others offered a few cents for return of clean bottles.

The dime admission brought an array of screen entertainment. We always arrived early and waited impatiently for the show to begin.

First, there were commercials for local business firms. Appearance of the first slide was the signal for bedlam to begin. Screams, shouts and whistles blended in a deafening uproar.

Everything quieted down when the Pathé News came on. This was the equivalent of the evening news capsules we get at dinner time on the modern television stations. The news program was sometimes preceded by a moving logo, a cameraman cranking a handle and swinging the camera around to confront the audience. The news portion usually featured photo coverage of breaking news only a few days old, with signing of treaties, floods, accidents, and beauty contests.

Then came the good stuff. A series of shorts which usually included a comedy, a cartoon comedy and the exciting serial. Our favorites in the first category were the "Our Gang" flickers, depicting the improbable and comic adventures of several youngsters: the fat kid, the tousled rube with the cowlick on his forehead, a black kid, sometimes a pretty little girl, and the dog. The latter was a sort of white mastiff with a ring painted around one eye.

The regular comedies usually featured Fatty Arbuckle and Harold Lloyd and later, Abbott and Costello. Star of the early cartoon comedies was Felix the Cat of the pre-Disney decades.

The serial was something else. It was an adventure series, which always ended with the heroine in dire peril. Like the girls bound with rope and left on the track of an oncoming train. Or the hero left dangling from the top of a railroad bridge. We could hardly wait until next week when the serial would resume.

The main movie, of course, was a cowboy film. The hero was usually Tom Mix. Sometimes we'd switch allegiance from the Majestic to the Wigwam, on West Second near Sierra, where Western heroes such as Hoot Gibson were stars.

I notice that nearly the same time as the Granada's demise was the closing of the best-known drive-in, the El Rancho at the Sparks border. I don't think El Rancho was the first drive-in hereabouts, but it was the longest-lived.

As time went on, the Wigwam was replaced by the Crest. A new theater appeared at South Virginia and Ryland, the Tower. Next door was a bowling alley, and movie patrons could hear the rumble and clatter of the balls and pins. —*September 29, 1993*

Carving up slices of culinary history
I guess you'd call it progress. Or growth.

At any rate, two of Reno's oldest landmark buildings are about to be no more. By the time this appears in print, both the Colombo and Toscano buildings will probably be demolished and the debris hauled away. They will be replaced by a parking lot.

Both buildings on the 200 block of Lake Street didn't add much to the scenery in recent years. In fact, they were downright frowzy.

But at one time, each of the adjacent buildings housed what were among the most popular restaurants in Reno.

Lake Street, particularly in the 1930s and '40s and before, hadn't become the Skid Row it was later labeled. There were a number of small hotels, cafes and shops in the downtown blocks of Lake. I know this because I delivered the Bay-area newspapers there every morning in the late '20s.

Rough-housing with the world heavyweight boxing champion, Max Baer at Al Tahoe. I made him holler: "Ouch! That's enough! — at least that's what I told my kids.

But for the ensuing decades, the Colombo was a standout Italian cafe and the Toscano was the first of the Basque enterprises. The upper floors of each were small hotels.

The Colombo had a huge bar room off its entrance and a big dining room encircled by booths and—on crowded nights—tables adjoining the small dance floor.

You could get a multicourse dinner at the Colombo during the days when Phil Curti operated it. And there was no cover charge for entertainment; the Colombo had a house band not only for dancing but to back up the nightly floor shows.

The shows were not elaborate, but for the price, the entertainment was as good as any you could find in Reno. Sometimes there was a dance pair doing the tango, a magician and assorted vocalists. And the band, led by Otillo Ravera, was great for dancing.

After Curti left the Colombo for the bowling business, it passed through various phases, the best of which was a Chinese food spot. In recent years it housed sleazy topless joints.

Next door was the Toscano, another place we recall with fondness for the great — and reasonable — Basque food. What a meal you got for $2; a platter of hors d'oeuvres, plus Basque (barley or tiny pastas) soup, beans, ravioli and french fries — and then your entree.

Unlike the Colombo, the Toscano had no dancing or entertainment. Its dining room had tables with private, curtained booths along the walls.

The Toscano had a large bar where people waited their turn to dine. Sometimes as many as 60 people were backed up.

The Toscano's heyday came in July of 1931 because of the Max Baer-Paulino Uzcudun fight, a 20-rounder at the racetrack, promoted and refereed by Jack Dempsey.

Paulino, the burly woodchopper from the Pyrenees Mountains of Spain, was the idol of his countrymen. And there were many Basques in Nevada. They came out of the sheep ranges, hills and ranches of Nevada and Idaho.

Uzcudun trained at Steamboat Springs, south of Reno, and the Basques trekked there to support him. They wore their traditional white shirts and trousers, with red belts or sashes, and red berets. And they all hung out at the Toscano.

Joe Elcano, Sr., was the best-known Toscano host, having reigned there for 25 years.

The east side of Lake Street, the two main downtown blocks, is becoming large concrete slabs. Long gone is the entire triangle block between First and Second streets, once the locale of various Chinese stores and a religious temple, or joss house.

Lone survivor of the next block, the 200, is the Pincolini Building which houses the Mizpah Hotel and appears to be in good shape.

In the adjacent 300 block, also long-departed, was Bill Fong's New China Club, the first interracial casino. In its time, it succeeded the ancient and sleazy Palm Saloon. All that area, too, is now parking lots—except for the former Railway Express office, which has been converted to a restaurant.

So much of that area is gone now, but we won't forget those great dinners at the Toscano and Colombo. —*April 29, 1987*

Silas E. Feemster was almost a legend in his own life at the University of Nevada

He was an eccentric professor in the days when only eccentric profs wore beards. Well, Silas E. Feemster had a close-cut beard and he WAS eccentric. He was almost a legend in his own life, at University of Nevada. He taught Ancient History, in a style which would horrify today's faculty.

My first day in his A.H. class began with his remarks about the Athenian's victory over the invading Persians at the battle of Marathon. After which one warrior, Pheidippides, ran all the way to the city, gasping with his last breath: "We have won the battle!" Whereupon, after a 24-plus mile run, he died.

"Why did he run? Why didn't he ride a horse," queried our professor. No one knew, so he dismissed the class.

Next day, the same question, the same no-nothing answer and again dismissal. After a while, we asked him. He explained that a certain kind of grass on which horses fed was lacking in Greece at that time.

One day his lecture wasn't taking effect, so he advised us to find the answer in the library. To illustrate this point, he left the class, walked across the street to the library. He returned with an armload of books, set them down, went across the street for another load.

At this point, the class bell rang and we all got out.

In the spring, Prof. Feemster got restless. He finished the lecture in the shade of a new-budding tree, on the lawn. Later he got more restless, and challenged us: "I can beat any guy in this class skipping stones."

Whereupon, we trooped to the shores of Manzanita Lake, scouting for flat stones. He always pitched for the faculty in the annual seniors-faculty game. And he could really skip those flat stones. But just then one of the large swans swam majestically into the line of fire. Feemster's stone bonked the waterfowl. There was a great squawking and flapping, and our game was over. The head groundskeeper came over and chewed out the professor. He got scolded the next day by the president,

There was a rumor that he disliked engineers, and flunked all the engineers in his class. After a protest they were reinstated.

I had a bad personal experience with him. Somehow I had slept through class time. However, when the other guys came down to our house at noon, they assured me that the Ancient History test was a snap. "And Feemster will certainly give you a re-X." Meaning a re-examination.

So, armed with excuses and prior knowledge, I approached the bewhiskered professor. He said sure he would give me a Re-X. Just two questions—give the history of Rome and the history of Athens.

I thought he was joking. "What part of Rome and Athens do you mean?"

"All you know about them."

So I tottered back to my desk. However, I was armed. We used blank sheaves of paper, both as a notebook and for exams. I had a notebook crammed with the histories of Rome and Athens. With the same light blue cover. I fiddled around with it for an hour—I knew the prof was restless. He stuffed my loose papers into his pocket and left. He had every pocket filled. The wind was blowing stiffly, and some of the papers blew all over the campus. We retrieved them.

When the grades came out, I got an "incomplete" in Ancient History. Couldn't raise Feemster on the phone. Desperate, I called Jeannie Weir, head of the department.

"Oh, Feemster has gone back to Nebraska for the summer," she advised, "and there is no phone on his farm." However, Miss Weir was able to contact someone on a neighboring farm, who brought Feemster to the phone.

"Oh, most of Cobb's papers blew out of the car while we were driving along the desert past Wendover." After a brief silence, he stated, "Give Cobb a B."

—August 13, 1995

We traveled the streets of Virginia City, lustily singing Yuletide carols

Is every Christmas alike? Not if you lived on the Comstock Lode years ago, like I remember. For one thing, it seems to me that there was more snow in the olden days. One other big difference is the Christmas trees, decorations, etc. In the early 1920s, we didn't have strings of vari-colored electrical lights for our trees. We used candles, which were held in small tin holders and which had to be lighted separately. It is a wonder that our house and the whole town didn't burn down!

Once my cat pulled over the entire tree, and luckily no candles were lighted at the time. She liked to play with the cotton ornaments that simulated vegetables. These looked like carrots, turnips, etc. The cat got a claw stuck in an ornament that she was batting around and pulled over the entire tree. We didn't have thin glass ornaments then.

> **A FORGOTTEN DELIVERY**
>
> *Sparks reader, Gunther Brueckner, is delighted with his newspaper delivery boy. The lad has laid the daily paper right on the porch, come rain or shine. Braved the worst snow storms to deliver the paper on time. Mr. Brueckner figured such diligence should be rewarded with a generous tip at Christmas time, a five-dollar bill. The lad was overjoyed. But the next day—for the very first time—there was no paper on the porch. Puzzled, the customer called the boy's house, reported the omission to the father. Found out the youngster was so delighted and excited with the generous gift that he completely forgot his benefactor's delivery—for the first and only time.*
>
> *—January 28, 1979*

My father often went out to get a Christmas tree and would bring home a piñon pine. These were very bushy and the branches were not as accessible as those on a regular pine or spruce.

The Christmas presents were the result of preliminary lobbying on the part of the child. We would spend a lot of time studying the toy section of the Sears, Roebuck and Montgomery Ward catalogs. Quite often we would take a pencil and encircle the description of a toy train, fake cowboy or soldier suit, mechanical trucks, etc. Then we would leave the catalog in a prominent place, open to the desired page, where perhaps an adult of the family would take notice.

For years I had a small windup train with a meager circle of track. Nothing like the dazzling Lionel or American Flyer electric trains in the catalog. One Christmas Eve, I was in bed and apparently sleeping when my parents checked. I heard a strange noise from the living room, got out of bed and opened the door. There was my Mom and Dad on their knees, playing with a brand-new electric train.

When they saw me staring at the sight, they arose and hustled me back to bed. I could hardly wait till morning, to be apparently surprised at what Santa had brought. Other surprise gifts sometimes included a new sled. Virginia City streets provided the best sledding in the world.

Another memory in my mind was a hay ride. This was back in 1930, when I was a sophomore at the Fourth Ward School. It had snowed considerably and the county had limited use of the lone plow. So the streets were well covered with snow. Someone obtained a huge dray, a freight-hauling vehicle on runners instead of wheels and was pulled by a two-horse team. The horses were attired in traditional sleigh bells. The bed of the vehicle was covered with hay and held about 20 of us high school students. In this we traveled the streets of Virginia City, lustily singing Yuletide carols.

During the Great Depression of the 1930s, even the churches suffered. One Christmas Eve, the only active church in town was the Catholic St. Mary's in the Mountains.

On Christmas Eve, people of all religious persuasions were welcome. So I, with a couple of friends, dressed up and set out for the ceremony. I believe Bill Marks Jr., Ed Colletti and Hobe Leonard were with me as we walked past the Crystal Bar. It was locked and the shutters closed. Mr. and Mrs. Marks Sr. had already gone done Taylor Street to the church. Bill Jr. remarked, "My dad left a big bowl of Tom 'n Jerrys on the bar...and I have the key!"

In a twinkling we were inside and lapped up a number of the delicious potent libations. Then we set out for St. Mary's. Unfortunately, it was very crowded and the usher seated us behind the big stove. There with the heat from the stove and from the Tom 'n Jerrys, we all fell asleep. The man passing the collection bag on the end of a long pole had to rap each of us on the head to stay awake.

—December 1988

Their brass fittings gleamed, and disgorged great clouds of black smoke from the coal or wood-burning engines

You're an Old-Timer if you remember when Commercial Row was Reno's main street.

Well, obviously no one is around who remembers the start of Commercial Row. That was back in 1868, when the townsite of Reno was laid out by surveyors for the Central Pacific Railroad.

Now, the once-bustling street is more of a back door for the big gambling casinos of downtown.

The five-block, one-side-only street has been absorbed by the Hilton (Flamingo), Fitzgeralds, Harolds and Harrah's. The west end is anchored by a big motel, the Colonial, but the rest is occupied by the casinos. And its very existence is threatened, if the Hilton can achieve its expansion northward.

Commercial Row has undergone many changes since it was laid out in '68. The centerpiece, the original surveyor's stake from which the townsite was laid out, is now occupied by the Sands Hotel on Third and Arlington.

Commercial Row was just what its name intended—a commercial street. It was first occupied by stores and hotels, adjacent to the railroad tracks and depots.

Old-time sketches and photos show the Depot Hotel prominent among the buildings.

Most of the hotels opposite the tracks and depot had large second-story balconies, from which flags waved and guests sat on chairs waving to passengers coming off the trains. And it was a popular area for parades.

There was a steady stream of transcontinental trains, pulled by the little locomotives with the inverted bell-shaped smokestacks, their brass fittings gleaming, disgorging great clouds of black smoke from the coal or wood-burning engines.

There was an original plan to have Commercial Row and the railroad tracks anchor a large plaza, or park, in the Mexican style. In fact, three blocks on the north side are still named "Plaza." Center Street was divided by warehouses and depots. The rebuilt depot has undergone many changes. Removal of the warehouse permitted opening of Center Street and University Avenue (to the University of Nevada campus) which was re-named North Center Street.

Prominent among the 19th-century business houses was the Novacovich building, dispenser of groceries and produce.

The southeast corner of Commercial Row and Center became the site of the Overland Hotel, a busy hostelry where the mining men and ranchers hung out. On the other corner, southwest, was the Palace Club whose second floor was occupied by the Palace Hotel.

The Palace hit its heyday during the time of the Johnson-Jeffries prize fight in July of 1910. The club was the ticket headquarters and the hangout for the press and fistic figures who came from all over the world.

Commercial Row, in general, thrived during the 1920s, '30s, and '40s. Most popular bistro was the Wine House, which featured a cafe and operated a huge bar, run by the Francovich family. Many Renoites today can recall the block between Virginia and Sierra streets as the site for Conant's grocery store, Cannan's Drug and Floral firm, Rauhut's Bakery, and other stores.

It was where the Horgan family operated the original Commercial Hardware, and there was a Reno Mercantile Co. farther west.

In this area were a number of small and popular taverns. Best known was Becker's. Many still around can recall getting their first beer at Becker's. —*August 23, 1989*

High jinks in the '30s

Well, the home football season is upon us.

The University of Nevada, Reno Wolf Pack will be playing here in Reno against its oldest opponent, University of Pacific, on Saturday. This rivalry goes back to 1898 when the first Nevada team beat the Stockton boys by 35 to zero. Pacific, then known as College of the Pacific (COP), figures frequently in Nevada football history.

An example is the 1919 game when the Nevada Sage Hens routed the Bengal Tigers by the greatest margin ever: 134-to-0. Then there's the notorious Revolution team which revolted againt the coach and, minus the coach, went to Stockton and got walloped, 51-0. Hank Clayton of Carson City proudly reminds us that Nevada spoiled the Amos Alonzo Stagg 50th anniversary fete by beating COP, by 8-0, in 1939. More recently, there was Eddie LeBaron's unforgettable performance for COP.

All of this leads up to the question, like Harry Belafonte's query: "Who took the ding-dong, who took the bell?" The answer is lost somewhere. There used to be a trophy for the winner of the annual Pacific-Nevada game. It was a big Sierra Pacific locomotive bell, loud when clanged.

One evening in the mid-1930s, a bunch of us were sitting around in the fraternity house, and the topic of the trophy bell came up. It seemed that Nevada hadn't gained possession of the bell for some time. One of the fellows revealed that he had learned the location of the once-prized trophy bell somewhere on the Stockton campus. Someone proposed that "We should get it back, and not wait for the football game outcome."

Accordingly, a raiding party was organized, and I was part of it. I believe we used Kenyon Richard's roadster to make the secret trip to

Stockton. Our informant said the trophy bell was kept at a certain fraternity house at COP.

Much later, we parked outside the bell's hideout. There was a lot of noise emanating from the place; it seems that the brothers were having a beer bust in their basement, and there was much singing and shouting from that cellar.

We stealthily entered the main door and found no one around. Following the tip, we went upstairs and in a rear storeroom found the trophy bell, all nicely crated in a wooden container. We removed it. But in the process of carrying it down the stairs, someone let part of the crate slip.

The bell and crate rolled down the stairs, clanging noisily at each step. We thought the racket would raise the entire fraternity, but only two young freshman pledges came up to investigate. We told them we were the rally committee and were taking the trophy bell downtown to the "rally." They not only were duped but helped us pack it out to the car. They helped put it in the rumble seat, never noticing the Nevada license plate.

Our return to Reno was triumphant, but the joy was shortlived. The Pacific administration protested sternly to the Nevada administration, which then equally sternly ordered us raiders to give it up.

Where is it now? —*September 8, 1992*

It was the first time mainland Japan had been attacked

We should never forget April 18, 1992, the 50th anniversary of the first U.S. air raid on the Japanese mainland. That's when Jimmy Doolittle led a flight of U.S. bombers from the USS Hornet on a mission which heartened all Americans. The squadron took off from the carrier, flew a great distance to the city of Tokyo and dropped American bombs on the Japanese metropolis.

Then the flyers continued to China, since they were getting low on fuel, and they landed there. Eventually, they found their way back to the U.S. forces. The sheer audacity of the historic raid captured the excitement of the American public, which had been glum since the cries of Japanese victories in the Pacific.

The reason I mention this historic raid, the first time the mainland of Japan had ever been attacked, is because of a Nevada connection.

My friend Selby Calkins of Reno has been reading the new biography of General Doolittle, and he noted with interest that the daring aviator had somewhat of a Nevada relationship.

It was in 1917 that Doolittle, a University of California student, came to Virginia City to take a summer job in the mines.

Strangely enough, Doolittle talked about his summers in the Comstock city but failed to mention an incident of note. Jimmy Doolittle was in Virginia City when tragedy struck. Two miners in the Union mine were dashed to their deaths when the cage (elevator) in which they were descending had a disastrous accident. The cage and the two miners plunged about 300 feet to the bottom of a shaft.

The unfortunate miners who were killed were George Benner (husband of my aunt, Mary Harris Benner) and Patrick "Paddy" Hughes. Both are buried in the Virginia City cemetery which adjoins the Union mine. The huge waste rock dump of the Union mine is very visible to motorists who come up the Geiger Grade and are within a mile of Virginia City.

At the time of the tragic mishap at the Union, the cage was unworkable, so a man was lowered to the bottom of the shaft to see if the miners had any chance of surviving the crash. A volunteer was selected for the task—Jimmy Doolittle.

Young Doolittle was lowered to the wreckage, but when he was hoisted back to the surface, he gave the sad news that both Benner and Hughes were dead. A few months after Doolittle gained his notoriety for the Tokyo raid, the late Delbert Benner, son of the mine accident victim, wrote to Gen. Doolittle to see if he remembered the incident. The general wrote back with a nice letter stating that he did, indeed, recall the accident and his exploit. Delbert's widow, Rene, had kindly forwarded to me a copy of the Doolittle letter.

Four-star Gen. Doolittle is 95 and lives in Pebble Beach, Calif. On the 50th anniversary of his daring raid on Tokyo, he had the good wishes of a nation whose spirits he lifted during the bleak days of 1942. —*April 1, 1992*

If Procter Hug started a carpet company, he could advertise: "Hug's Rugs"

Once there was a publicity director at Fresno State College with the rhyming name of Channing Manning.

This intrigued many persons, including the sports writers with whom Mr. Manning dealt during his duties. One of these was Prescott Sullivan of the *S.F. Examiner*, who happened to be on a train passing through the town of Banning, Calif. He cooked up a column item about how nice it would be if there was a canning company in Banning. And with Channing Manning as its owner or president. Putting them together, the names would form "Channing Manning Canning in Banning."

Over the years, we have savored this item, and often thought about what charming combinations some of our own local names would make.

We often thought how Louis Spitz and Art Spatz would make ideal business partners, perhaps manufacturing spatulas. Think of "Spitz-Spatz Spiffy Spatulas!"

If attorney Joe Key and son, attorney Jon Key, went into the locksmith business, they'd have a snappy sign: "Key-Key Key Co."

If Preston Hale left real estate and started a bail bond firm, he'd have a nice sign: "Hale Jail Bail."

In these poetic fantasies, we have in mind the ladies who work as receptionists or phone-answerers for various local firms, and answer incoming calls with their offices' official names. Some are tongue-twisters, as it is, and we think musical combinations would make their tasks easier.

Like if Larry Taylor went into the tailor profession, and specialized in Navy uniforms, it'd be: "Taylor, Sailor Tailor."

If John Hiskey was in the liquor business, he could advertise: "Frisky Hiskey Whiskey."

Ex-district attorney Larry Hicks and his brother Bud formed their own law firm. If Paul Hickey got a law degree, they could take him into the firm of "Hicks, Hickey, Hicks."

Suppose that Carl Felten and Rollan Melton got into the ore smelting business, and took in Russ Sheldon as a partner? "Felten, Melton & Sheldon, Smelting." That's got rhythm.

If Procter Hug started a carpet company, he could advertise: "Hug's Rugs."

And Eddie Hill should be a pharmacist, with a sign that reads: "Hill's Pills."

Suppose Norman Dain sold drains? And if "Dain Rain Drain Co." became a chain of stores? You get the idea.

There are plenty of promising usable names around this paper's newsroom. We could set up editor Robert Ritter in a specialty cafe selling "Ritter's Fritters"...and put Ev Landers in the loan business: "Landers, Lender"... and if Bob Nitsche had been a dermotologist instead of an editor, we'd have a slogan for his firm: "Feet Itchy? See Nitsche"... if John Irby opened a hat store, with Ed Kirby, they could feature the "Irby-Kirby Derby"...And publisher Warren Lerude could open a music store as "Lerude Etude." (Now that's musical.)

If Clarence Jones went in for paleontology, his business card could read tersely, "Jones, Bones."

And maybe Howard Zink could become a psychiatrist. His card would read, simply, "Zink, Shrink."

If James Herz became a furrier, he'd advertise "Herz Furs."

How about band leader Fred Nagel? He should buy out a bakery and feature "Nagel's Bagels."

How about Alex Glock Fixing Clocks?

Don't know if Bob Rusk and Joe Lusk are acquainted, but they'd be a good team for marketing musk-scented husks. Try that on your telephone: "Rusk-Lusk's Musk Husks."

Let's set up Harvey Rose in a photography studio. "Rose's Poses" would be catchy.

Here's a natural: Let warehouseman Frank Bender start an auto body repair shop. If you suffered a fender bender, you could see "Bender, the fender mender."

The word "park" has a lot of new uses of late. They even call an auto parking lot a park. So why shouldn't erstwhile Tahoe hotelman Brooks Park call his parking lot the "Park's Park Park?"

Then if Chris Ault and Nolan Gault started an insurance firm, their title would hav a ring to it: "Ault & Gault, No-Fault."

What if Don Heath and Karl Keith were dentists? They'd have a simple sign: "Heath & Keith, Teeth." Maybe Murray Moler could join the firm.

Now if there was a jello plant owned by assemblyman Don Mello: Mello Jello. And if you asked about the product, the operator could tell you: "Mello's Jello, mellow, fellow."

A good rhyming title for a grog shop owned by Marc Picker would be: Picker, Liquor.

Someone could do something with a fictitious post: Ex-Silver Sox manager Eddie Watt going to work for Sierra Pacific Power. Or with Sox general manager Harry Platt becoming associated with the county surveyors: "Platt's plats," etc.

Let's create a mythical book store, operated by UNR track coach Jack Cook. Cook's Books? And if he specialized in cookbooks—well, you get the idea.

For the marketing of Oriental gongs, we can envision a merger of Bill Fong, Art Long, Cam Tong and Benny Wong as associates. Let's hear it for the "Wong-Fong-Tong-Long Gong Co." Bong!

Now this one should ring a chime, especially if it specializes in manufacture and distribution of bells. Let's form a partnership involving Vance Bell, Bob Ring, Peter Ting and April Ringer. Are you ready for "Ring, Ting Tinger and Bell, Bells?"

Let's put together Bob Best and Louis Test in an eradication service which could be dubbed: "Best & Test Pest."

Police reporter Phil Barber could open a barber shop: "Barber, Barber."

And if George Basta would switch from fuel oil to a spaghetti-macaroni shop? Call it "Basta Pasta."

Now, if Roy Powers and Bob Bowers opened a florist shop, the receptionist could have ear-pleasing response: "Powers & Bowers, Flowers."

Of course the ideal space-sharing office should involve a Reno phrenologist and a proctologist. Then the answering service could inquire: "Heads or Tails?" —*May 25, 1980*

Only 1950s fans will remember a second-sacker for the Silver Sox

You're an Old Timer if you remember that the present Atlanta Braves' manager was once a Reno Silver Sox player.

Only the fans who were around Moana in the 1950s will remember Bobby Cox as a second-sacker for the Silver Sox. Now he's the field pilot for the Braves, who just fired their latest manager.

Actually, being a big-league manager is nothing new to Cox. He formerly piloted the Atlanta teams, then led the Toronto Blue Jays to success, before returning to Atlanta in a front-office post. After being groomed at Reno in the 1950s, Bobby Cox went up to the Dodgers, then played a lot of third base for the Yankees.

Unless I've missed something, Jim Lefebvre has been manager of Seattle, and he was also a second-sacker for Reno in the California League.—July 1, 1990

Heavy make-up, heady perfume

Does your conscience trouble you long after you did something not quite right? How about half century later?

Even now, after 50 years, when I pass along Commercial Row in Reno, a twinge of memory is felt. Now, the massive Harrah's complex occupies most of two blocks of Commercial Row between Virginia and Lake streets. But back in the early 1930s, those blocks were crammed with saloons/gambling joints, stores, fortune tellers' stalls, and other enterprises.

Including a "Taxi Dance" place.

A "Taxi Dance" had nothing to do with taxicabs. It was a dance hall where the customer paid a young (not always) woman a fee of a dime for a whirl on the dance floor.

Back around 1933, with two high school buddies from Virginia City, we came to Reno for some purpose or other and were strolling along the sidewalk of Commercial Row when we heard the strains of music from above. It came from a second-floor establishment, where the toe-tickling music of a saxophone, a drum and a piano provoked the interest of passers-by.

Having no experience in this line, we three lads from the mining camp were intrigued. After some fidgeting at the downstairs door, we decided to take a hasty whirl at the dime-a-dance thing. Perhaps we might pick up a new dance step or two with which to impress the hometown girls.

At the top of the stairs a man at a desk shoved a handful of little tickets—the kind you get for raffles or amateur entertainment—at us. Each of we three teenagers hooked up with a partner in evening gown, heavy make-up and heady perfume. As we guided or shuffled across the slick floor, we entered small-talk with the ladies, most of which consisted of their remarks about our talent of "natural rhythm," etc. And the advice that several more dances would straighten out any flaws we mighthave.

I was nervously thinking of our dwindling supply of dimes, when one of the ladies loudly announced she was "so thirsty" and suggested we all have a drink. One of my buddies, Delbert Benner, looked warily at me, and I looked likewise at our third friend, Albert Avansino. Albert (Abe) was a handsome lad, already working on a Clark Gable mustache, and a buoyant personality. To our dismay, he agreed to the suggestion and we all headed for a booth, where we all ordered cooling drinks.

One of the dance partners doubled as a waitress. Strangely, each of the dance ladies ordered "the usual" which looked strangely like ice tea. This was quickly downed, and each ordered another. And another. (There must have been a run on Hills Brothers or Lipton's Tea that week.)

Alarmed, I muttered to Del Benner that we were getting in deep, and whispered, "Who's going to pay for this?"

"Oh, I guess Avansino wants to pay for everything," he ventured.

About this time, the hostesses took a break.

This gave us a chance to ask Avansino when he was going to pay our bill. Dismayed, he informed us he thought "Benner or Cobb had the money!"

This precipitated our next move. Ostensibly heading for the gents' john, we strolled near the doorway. And down the stairs we fled!

Taking the steps at two or three at a time, we reached the street to the accompaniment of angry shouts from the manager and his bouncer. We fled past the Southern Pacific depot, across the railroad tracks and into a parking lot, with the angry "enforcers" in hot pursuit. Each of us rolled under a car in the parking lot, while the posse from the dime-a-dance hall searched for the fugitives.

One of them had been brandishing a "billy club" the last glimpse we had of him. We quivered in fear as the rough guys roamed up and down the lines of cars, mouthing loud threats about the bloody punishment they would wreak on the cheapskates who had stiffed the establishment.

Fortunately, they tired of the search and returned to the Taxi Dance quarters.

The cheapskates, or suckers—Avansino, Benner and Cobb—eventually crawled out from beneath the parked cars and departed.

Even now, 50 or so years later, even with the sleazy Taxi Dance joint long gone and replaced by the modern Harrah's structures, I have a twinge of memory. —*December 16, 1984*

Postscript

Ty Cobb passed away on Sunday, May 25, 1997. The following four columns, his last, were originally to appear in the final weeks before the publication of this book. They were printed together in the *Reno Gazette-Journal*, as part of a tribute, on Sunday, June 1, along with the accompanying piece by his long-time friend and colleague, Rollan Melton.

The Final Page: Nevada journalism legend Ty Cobb leaves behind his final words of humor and wisdom

He was physically frail, and his eyes were blinded by glaucoma, and yet he was fired by the competitive spirit that galvanized him in a Nevada journalism career that endured for six decades.

But there was his personal pride, a reserve strength, noble institutional memory and his vow to go out as he came in—as a writer—that enabled Ty Cobb to compose the four farewell columns readers see here.

He initially intended that the columns appear on successive Sundays in the *Reno Gazette-Journal*, concluding June 15. At 81, he was hanging up his newspaper gloves, to paraphrase a sports cliché. He had his last columns scheduled to coincide with the completion of his book, *The Best of Cobbwebs*. He would be at a gala autograph party that final Sunday.

His farewell words were crafted in his darkness just as were all the columns h& wrote in recent years. Unless you were around him in that period, you'd have not guessed his predicament.

He never told readers his eyes were shot, and he didn't wish that loss advertised by others. He wanted to take what was, accept it, and find joy in the blessings of family, home and friends.

He didn't say it in so many words, but Ty Cobb remained to his death, last Sunday, May 25, a man who regarded each day as Thanksgiving.

The Ty Cobb subjects and careful writing you see here are typical of the millions of published words he churned out in Reno since his University of Nevada graduation in 1937.

He talks here of himself, yet in his familiar manner that compels us to identify with the times, the characters, the life of the Nevadans. There is history here for new Nevadans, and invigorating historical reprises for long-timers. There is Ty Cobb's gorgeous storytelling gift, and there is classic humor—I bet you'll bust out laughing when you read what Reno mayor E. F. Roberts squawked at a grounded eagle.

To the conclusion of his beautiful, fruitful life, he kept active. Last Saturday, Memorial Day weekend, he hiked the cemeteries at Virginia City, Dayton and Reno to say good-bye to his Irish ancestors and lost friends.

His "Kids on the Comstock" speech a few days earlier at Virginia City attracted many more people than there were seats, to his delight. Ty Cobb, rejuvenated at being home on the Comstock with dear friends, chanted history and humor for two straight hours.

It was his way of saying good-bye.

The incomparable old sportswriter had done his meritorious best in a career that lasted a Nevada record, 60 years.

Now, the great warrior was going out on his own terms.

What you see on these pages is what he did best. Creating words that painted pictures, informed, stimulated and tickled.

All for the love of people.

Rollan Melton

The final four

A few months back I announced that I would be ending this column, wrapping up a career that began 60 years ago. It's a tough decision— I've really enjoyed writing this column, which I started in 1965 and has been running for more than 32 years—which works out to over 3,700 columns! But it's getting tougher to pound out my weekly words of wit and wisdom on my trusty Underwood manual typewriter (does anybody else, still use them?).

I plan to write a few final columns, leading up to the publication of my book, *The Best of Cobbwebs,* that will be out in June. Since so many of you have enjoyed the stories about the "good old days"' in Virginia City and Reno, I thought I'd reflect now a bit about those times and the things about these two great towns that stick in my memory.

I grew up in Virginia City, where I was born in 1915. By that time my family had lived on the Comstock for more than six decades. My grandparents were among the first to come to the Comstock back in the 1860s. My paternal grandfather, George Cobb, had served in the Civil War, enlisting from Tennessee in the Union Army (that's right, the Union) at the tender age of 15, joining the Cavalry troops. George had a short but lively war experience. He was badly wounded in action, wound up as a Confederate prisoner, escaped, and after the war came West to find his fortune in the mines. George was smitten by Mary Mahoney, an Irish lass who was already living in Dayton. It's amazing that Mary ever made it to America. Her first attempt at a transatlantic crossing ended up a disaster— she was shipwrecked and floated for days in the Irish Sea before being rescued. After they married, George worked as a laborer, and miner. He and Mary had three sons—George, Sam and Will, my dad. After Mary was widowed, she fell on hard times and the brothers were placed in various orphanages in the area, and later in Grass Valley, Calif.

On my mom's side, mother Eva was one of eight children of Richard and Jeanette Harris. Richard had emigrated from Cornwall, England, where many of the miners were recruited—the famous "Cousin Jacks." Richard worked mainly at the Yellow Jacket mine, where he narrowly escaped death from the terrible fire in the 1870s that killed 47 miners.

He met and married Jeannette Simpson, whose own family had come over from Scotland and wound up in Virginia City about 1863. Jeanette's father, George, was a skilled stone mason who laid the foundations of many of the big mines and churches that are still standing today. Her mother, Catherine Forbes Simpson, died around 1886 and is buried in Virginia City's cemetery.

My parents, Will and Eva, were an interesting couple, being so opposite in temperament and lifestyles. Before they married, Will was a true roundabout, somewhat undisciplined, aggressive, a boy who loved sports, fighting and good times. He was a talented baseball player, playing a number of positions for the Dayton team when he lived there.

Eva was prim and proper, reserved and quiet. But something struck, and they married in 1913. I was born two years later in the house they lived in down below the mine dumps on the Northeast edge of Virginia City.

My dad, Will, abandoned the wildness of his youth and became more like my mom every day—quiet, reserved, content to stay at home after work. Home for us was a two-story house southeast of town. I can remember the coyotes that hung out around us. We later moved up to C Street, about a half mile south of the Presbyterian church. That house is still there and I think it is now Maggie's Antiques.

———————

Growing up in Virginia City in the '20s was a great experience. The town's economy was doing well—not the booming bonanza of the 1800s to be sure, when the town had 35,000-40,000 residents—but fairly prosperous. A few of the mines, like the Yellow Jacket, the Con Virginia and California (the C&C), were still operating and that fueled the town's economy.

My dad, Will, was a miner, and later worked in various jobs, including an aerial tramway that carried ore from the mines down to the Butter's Plant by Sugarloaf Mountain. After an accident there, he switched to driving the stage from Virginia City to Dayton, then took over the Reno run. Later he drove his Marlin coach every day from Virginia City to Reno, over to Carson, up to South Tahoe to Glenbrook, Zephyr Cove, Bijou, Al Tahoe and Camp Richardson and back. He did that for 40 years, and you know what the roads were like then.

Will also served 12 years in the Nevada Assembly and Senate, where he wielded rare power in the Legislature. Being elected an independent, he found himself cloaked with tie-breaking powers. He was later elected sheriff of Storey County and a county commissioner.

Eva was a homemaker who participated in many civic activities in Virginia City. She also worked for many years as an attaché in the Nevada Legislature.

You might be interested in knowing what Virginia City looked like in the 1920s. If you came into "VC" up the old Gold Hill grade and over the Divide, the Fourth Ward School was on your right. Originally opened in 1876, the school housed all grades from elementary through high school. Along C Street you would go by Mrs. Eddy's little shop, full of needles, thread, candy—you name it. There was the Tahoe Restaurant, Prater's Grocery, the stylish Washoe Club where the rich miners hung out, and the old firehouse. Crossing Taylor street you came by Bill Mark's unique Crystal Bar, then full of the most amazing machines and paraphernalia.

Along C Street there was the Union Butcher Shop, John Terkla's Pastime Club, the Old Sawdust Corner, and a Chinese restaurant where Don McBride's "Bucket of Blood" now stands. Angelo Petrini's Delta Saloon was then known as The Smokery, a local bar and card parlor operated by Joe Viani. It was one of the few places we teen-agers could go in—we played pool in the back.

Further down you passed Sam Mariani's Grocery, the Brass Rail Bar and the notorious Union Bar run by Bronco Lazzeri. Up on B Street was the county Court House, where Justice is not blind, and the famed Piper's Opera House. The landmark International Hotel between C and B Streets on Union (where my father's mother had worked as a maid) had already tragically burned to the ground.

The Virginia City phone switchboard was next to a bakery where my mother worked. Calls were skillfully transferred by Suzie Davis, who moved plugs from hole to hole to connect us all without fail. Amazing when you consider she was blind! She recognized the callers by the sounds made by tabs that fell from the board when someone called "central."

Reminiscing about the old days on the Comstock reminds me of a funny story. Looking for some excitement, three Comstock cousins—me, Delbert Benner, and Glen Harris—decided we'd find it in a buggy ride down Virginia City's streets. We commandeered a horse buggy and stripped it down to its bare essentials, hauled it up Union Street above the Opera House, and jumped on. Bad decision.

We careened wildly across B Street, then C—fortunately no cars were coming—scattered some Indians playing cards near D Street, sailed out of control over the V&T tracks and finally crashed outside a Chinese Joss House down below F Street. No one was badly hurt, at least until our parents got hold of us. The county commissioners were moved to pass an ordinance the next day outlawing buggy riding on VC's streets. That was hardly necessary, from our point of view.

My cousin Delbert was a great guy. Some of you may remember him as the heart of the Virginia City Volunteer Fire Department. Delbert never knew his dad, who was killed in a cage (elevator) accident at the Union mine when Delbert was just a year old. The town knew that two miners were still in the mine and two young men volunteered for the dangerous rescue try. Down the hoist they went and found the miners, but both were dead.

My dad was one of the two brave rescuers. The other was a young engineering student from the University of California named Jimmy Doolittle. Yes, that was the same fellow who became the famous General Doolittle, the great aviator who led the daring World War II raid on Tokyo.

When the Depression hit, life in VC became much more difficult. Most of the mines closed and work was very hard to find. We had no more newspapers, no sports or other activities in school—except basketball. Canceling high school basketball on the Comstock was never going to happen. But we had no band, no music, no diversions. Times got very tough.

———————

Our family moved to Reno in the late 1920s so my dad Will could be closer to the start of the stage run he drove. We lived over on Wheeler Avenue for about three years. I went to Southside Elementary, where the city hall is located along Center Street. I also attended Northside Junior High, a site now occupied by the Bowling Stadium.

The event I most remember from that era was Charles Lindbergh flying into Reno. At the time the so-called airport was what is now the 5th Fairway of the Washoe Golf Course. The famed "Lone Eagle" brought his Spirit of St. Louis in for a landing and the crowd went wild.

There was a ceremony presided over by Reno's Mayor, E. E. Roberts, who had an eagle inside a cage that was supposed to bravely fly out to freedom when the door was unlocked. Instead the bird just sat in there, infuriating a somewhat inebriated Mr. Mayor, who was heard to shout at the recalcitrant eagle, "Fly, you son of a bitch, fly." It didn't. Hizzoner then startled the crowd by whacking the poor bird with his cane.

In 1933, I entered the University of Nevada. There were probably 1,000 students enrolled then, almost all of us struggling to get by in those Depression times. I decided to major in history and English, but my first love from the beginning was journalism (you couldn't major in that yet). The department was really one man—the venerable Prof. Al Higginbotham.

I joined the Sigma Nu fraternity. It was on Center Street just down from the campus' main entrance. What a dingy place our frat house was. One bathtub, no shower, very little furniture. But a great group of guys lived there—Stan Smith, Oly Glusovich, Bill Beemer, the Blakely brothers, Ray Armstrong, Ross Tannehill, Roy Gomm, Cliff Quilici, Whit DeLaMare, Olinto Barsanti, Tom Beko and others crammed into that place.

As much as I wanted to get into journalism, when I graduated there were no jobs to be found. So I went back to Virginia City and started working around the mines again. I worked on the old Crown Point Trestle in Gold Hill, helping tear it down. Almost fell off once and would have gone down about 90 feet, but luckily when I threw my sledgehammer forward, I was able to regain my balance. That was tough work for $5 a day, but what else was there?

Then the *Nevada State Journal* called and offered me a starting position. I jumped at it, but after working 60 hours a week and getting paid only $15, I decided to go back to the Comstock. The Journal upped the offer to $17.50 and the rest, as they say, is history. Sixty years later I'm still writing a column for the Journal.

The Journal was located then across from the old City Hall on Center Street. On one side of the Journal was Eddie Vacchina's Alpine Saloon. On the other was the infamous "Dog House," where my then-girlfriend, a Chinese fan dancer, worked.

I could hear the music from the club blaring through the thin walls. When intermission came, I would sneak into the alley and flirt with her. Later the Journal moved across the street and merged printing operations with the rival *Reno Evening-Gazette.*

At the Journal I did all of the beats from printer's assistant to city desk to sports. You had to be versatile. Not having a car, I often hitched a ride from the university on board an open-air garbage truck which detoured by the Journal to drop me off. Despite my fragrancy, I later became the sports editor and held that position for 22 years.

In 1939 1 married Olga Glusovich of Tonopah. We first lived above what old-timers will remember as the Penguin Cafe on South Virginia Street, now an Italian restaurant. Being orphaned early in life, Olga had a tough childhood. My six-day-a-week work schedule did not make life any easier for her.

After the war, Reno grew into a city of 30,000-35,000 folks and, in my mind, was a very classy town. I think Reno reached its heyday in the 1950s what a great place. The skyline, such as it was, was dominated by the towering, 12-story Mapes hotel, superseding the six-story skyscraper the El Cortez Hotel.

Chet and Link Piazzo opened their Sportsman store on Virginia Street just north of the tracks, across from the popular college hangout, the Little Waldorf. The Big Waldorf was a classy restaurant on

Virginia. The Club Fortune and Leon 'n' Eddies were on Second Street where the Cal Neva is now.

The Town House with its dance floor and band was across from where the Granada is, and Tony's El Patio Spanish Ballroom ("Swing & Sweat with Tony Pachett") was at Commercial Row and Chestnut (Arlington). The Coney Island Bar was a popular spot, as was The Wolf Den by the University.

I remember the French Bakery at Plaza and Virginia and Bello's, where you would get tamales from the basement window; the Wigwam with its apple pie; Margaret Burnam's coffee shop, Tiny's Waffle Shop, Becker's Bar and Gee's Chinese Pagoda in Sparks.

Johnny's Little Italy was originally in an alcove between the Mapes and Majestic Theaters. Speaking of theaters, remember the Crest and the Tower?

Over on Sierra Street were the main department stores—Montgomery Wards, JC Penney, Sears Roebuck and the National Dollar Store. The Folk & Campbell Shoe store was on Second; Brick's, Patterson's and Herd & Short were stylish men's stores. Joseph Magnin was downtown, too.

Wingfield Park had the same tennis courts of today, but were bordered by the Truckee, which was slowed by a series of small dams. Idlewild had it its little zoo that housed some poor, hapless bears and a log cabin-style pool house. Virginia Lake, constructed during the Depression—as was the Washoe Golf Course by the WPA—had yet to be overwhelmed by geese and seagulls. Most elementary kids attended mission style schools (e.g., Mt. Rose) and there were only three high schools. Yep, Reno was a great place to live then.

After more than 60 years in journalism I am saying farewell to a career that has been the focus of my life. It has allowed me to rub shoulders with presidents and with boxers sporting cauliflower ears. I have covered college basketball games in Madison Square Garden and high school football games in Battle Mountain. I have reported on the World Series and kept statistics at Little League games.

Journalism has changed dramatically over the years. I always tried to emphasize the positive in the subjects of my stories, especially sports.

I am asked why I liked sports so much. My answer is found in the belief that the love of the game usually brought out the best in the athlete. I have been fortunate to have known some of the best of the best—Jim Thorpe, Jesse Owens, Marion Motley, Archie Moore and of course my namesake, the Georgia Peach, Tyrus Raymond Cobb.

I have many to thank for my success in the field, and it is incumbent upon me to start with my late wife Olga. She endured many hardships—not only financial from the meager pay we made at the paper but putting up with my being gone long hours away from home. Olga's parents both died before she was 6. To a great extent she raised herself, but the folks in Tonopah, the Beko family, in particular, were wonderful to her. And she was wonderful to me—we had over 50 great years before she passed away three years ago.

As I mentioned in the last column, we first lived over the Penguin Cafe, later moving to a house on Claremont Street which had, at most, 800 square feet. By 1950 we had three kids—Ty Jr., Patricia and Bill

My duties as sports editor kept me away from home a great deal, and the responsibility of raising the family fell on Olga. I like to think she did a pretty good job. I will never forget the many publishers, editors and reporters with whom I worked—great people like John Sanford, Joe Jackson, Clarence Jones, Paul Leonard, Rollie Melton, Dick Schuster, Len Crocker, Sharon Genung, Frank Sullivan and others.

When I was sports editor I also churned out a column, Inside Stuff. It was my dear friend Rollie who later suggested in 1965 that I write a general interest column that became Cobbwebs.

As I noted a little while back, with the assistance of the UNR Foundation, C. J. Hadley, the Black Rock Press and countless others, we have extracted 150 or so of my better columns for inclusion in *The Best of Cobbwebs*, which is due to be distributed this month. Hopefully you will find it of interest. All proceeds go to the University.

My colleagues and contemporaries have been generous to me over the years with awards and recognition's. I have been inducted in several

Halls of Fame -- the Virginia City Alumni, the World Boxing Hall, the Wolf Pack and others.

But my most cherished award is one that comes from my roots, the University's Distinguished Nevadan Award. My columns reflect my love of Nevada and the heritage I have appreciated dating back to the 1860s when my great-grandparents came to this state.

Home Means Nevada to me. So it is, having entered the ninth decade of my life and after 60 years at the Journal, I'm "hanging up my spikes" —or in this case, my trusty old Underwood. And now I conclude my career with the traditional reporter's sign-off ...

— 30 —

The Author

Ty Cobb was born in Virginia City, Nevada in 1915. After grammar school on the Comstock, his family moved to Reno where he attended Northside Junior High School. Returning to Virginia City, he graduated from the Fourth Ward School. College years were spent at the University of Nevada where he was a member of Sigma Nu fraternity and graduated with a degree in English. He began working for the *Nevada State Journal* as a reporter in 1938. After stints as sports editor and managing editor, he retired as the paper's associate editor in 1975. His well-known column, *Cobbwebs,* began in 1965, and over 3,000 have been published.

Over the years Ty received numerous awards, including the Nevada Press Association's "Silver Makeup Rule," its highest honor; induction into the Nevada Wolf Pack's Hall of Fame; and the University of Nevada's Distinguished Nevadan award.

Designed by Robert E. Blesse.
The typeface is Adobe Garamond.
Printed by Edwards Brothers
of Ann Arbor, Michigan.